bullying

What adults need to know and do to keep kids safe

PEOPLE SAFETY
kidpower
SOLUTIONS

Irene Van der Zande

kidpower
PRESS

Copyright Information

Bullying - What adults need to know and do to keep kids safe Copyright © 2010 by Irene van der Zande All rights reserved. No part of this book may reproduced or copied in any manner without prior written permission of the author, except for brief quotations in reviews.

Use of Material. Readers are encouraged to use ideas from this book and other Kidpower educational materials in their personal and professional lives. We ask that readers give proper acknowledgement to Kidpower Teenpower Fullpower International when they use any examples, ideas, stories, language, or practices that they learned from our program and let others know how to reach our organization – without giving the impression they are authorized or certified by our organization unless they truly are. For any questions about acknowledgement or use, please e-mail safety@kidpower.org or call (o) 1-831-426-4407 extension 1#.

Restrictions. Individuals and groups must have an active certification or agreement with Kidpower Teenpower Fullpower International to be authorized to teach, promote, or organize workshops or other presentations using the Kidpower, Teenpower, Fullpower, or People Safety program names, workshop names, reputation or credentials. Please visit **www.kidpower.org** or call our office for information about our instructor certification and center development programs.

Disclaimer. Each situation and individual is unique and neither the author nor Kidpower can make any guarantee about the safety or effectiveness of the content or techniques described in this book. We do not accept responsibility for any negative consequences from the use or misuse of this information.

Publisher Kidpower Teenpower Fullpower International
P.O. Box 1212, Santa Cruz, CA, 95061, U.S.A; (o) 1-831-426-4407 Ext. 1#;
safety@kidpower.org **www.kidpower.org**

Graphic Design and Layout. Thank you to Ian Price of Price Watkins for our Kidpower logo and this book cover and design. www.pricewatkins.com

A Dedication to My Family

Kidpower would simply not exist without the love, generosity, and help of the members of my family and this book is dedicated to them:

To my husband Ed who has given me and Kidpower constant unwavering support, our two children Chantal and Arend who brought me into this work, and our joyous granddaughter Svea who keeps me doing it.

To my parents Raim and Lily who taught me to do good in the world, put important things into writing, and be true to myself. To my sister Elaine and brother Ken, for every phone call, email and early morning walk.

I also want to honor the memory of our longtime family friend, Eve, who passed away at the age of 95. Over cups of steaming tea and perfect soft-boiled eggs, Eve provided endless faith that Kidpower would flourish, even during the most challenging times.

And, finally this book is also dedicated to the countless individuals who have made a commitment to become part of our growing Kidpower family over the past 21 years. To each of you, I give my deepest thanks for all you do to make our organization strong and our services exceptional.

Foreword by Ellen Bass

I have known Irene van der Zande for well over twenty-five years and feel proud to be a longtime Kidpower supporter. Irene and I met the day our daughters entered kindergarten. We sat next to each other in tiny child-size chairs as our children took this large step into the world.

We got to know each other better when Irene started a Girl Scout troop. She was a wonderful and original Girl Scout leader. Our troop didn't sell cookies, but the girls and their families had fun, learned a lot, stayed safe, and, despite our many differences, treated each other with respect. Very much like Kidpower.

Kidpower came into being and thrives because of Irene's vision, creativity, joy in life, courage, integrity, and love. All of these qualities are integrated on every level of the Kidpower program and organization.

For example, in the Kidpower office, Irene has instructed the staff not to answer the telephone or even an email unless they are prepared to be fully present for each person on the other end of the communication. If you're rushed or distracted, it's okay to let the machine take a message, she tells them. The goal is to have every interaction be a model of respect and helpfulness.

Like Irene, Kidpower walks its talk. This integrity creates a culture where people sustain a deep commitment to quality and keep looking for ways to improve what they do. The values of the organization are not just on paper but embodied in each decision, class, and relationship.

Kidpower is committed to respect for everyone, reaching out to people who are most vulnerable to violence and abuse, as well as those who have traditionally been oppressed or excluded.

Finally, the Kidpower method works. A few years ago, my niece, who is developmentally delayed, participated in the Kidpower program. She'd been harassed by a man in her workplace and was feeling frightened and upset. With just two empowering Kidpower sessions, she was confident about her ability to protect herself. When we walked out of the training, she turned to me and said, "I feel like I've just gotten a new life."

For years, I have been telling Irene that she needed to write a book for all the people who haven't been to a class as well as for the ones who have. I'm so glad she's finally taken my advice! Her writing is easy to read, interesting, and useful. I hope that you will find inspiration and guidance in how to bring Kidpower to the young people in your life.

Ellen Bass
Co-Author of *The Courage to Heal and Free Your Mind*
Founding Kidpower Board President

Contents

Dedication 3
Foreword 4
Note From the Author 9

Chapter One
Bad News and Good News About Bullying 10

Chapter Two
Some Facts About Bullying 12
    According to Our Experts – What Our Students Tell Us 12
    According to Ken Rigby, Ph.D. 13
    What the Research Means for Caring Adults 14
    Times Have Changed 14
    How Do People Bully? 15
Ideas for Discussing Bullying with Children 16

Chapter Three
What Makes Bullying Hard to Stop? 17
    Most Babies Come With Everything 17
    Why Do People Bully? 18
    Whether Behavior is Bullying or Leadership Can Depend
        on the Rules 19
    But It's Just a Joke! 20
    From the Mouths of "Innocents" 21
    Victim Behavior 21
    Prejudice 22
    Poor Adult Role Models 23
    Acceptance That This Is Just the Way Things Are 24
    Peer Orientation 25
Ideas for Dealing with Issues That Make Bullying Hard to Stop ... 26

Chapter Four
Managing Emotional Triggers to Prevent Explosions ... 27
    Emotional Safety Techniques to Deal With Bullying ... 27
    Get Specific 28
    Taking the Power Out of the Word "Crybaby" 29
    Reframing the Word "Bitch" 31
    The "Asshole" Success Story 32
    But What if We Both Like It? 33
    Staying in Charge of Your Body and Your Words 34
Teaching Children to Manage Their Emotional Triggers ... 35

Chapter Five
Target Denial to Avoid Trouble 36
    What is Target Denial? 36
    Noticing Potential Trouble 36
    Don't Be There 37

The Have-a-Nice-Day! Self-Defense Tactic 37
What *Most* Mothers Prefer 38
Walking Past Trouble 38
The Fallacy of "Giving As Good As You Get" 39
Practicing Using Target Denial to Prevent Bullying 39

Chapter Six
Conflict Resolution and Interventions to Solve Problems **40**
What Is Meant by "Conflict Resolution" 40
What Is a Mediator? 41
Negotiation Buddies 42
When Adults Don't Do Anything 42
Mixed Messages 43
Interventions to Prevent Conflict From Escalating 43
Teaching Young People How to Use Conflict Resolution Skills 45

Chapter Seven
Self-Protection Skills to Avoid Being Pushed, Tripped, Bumped, Hit, Kicked, or Shoved **46**
Making the Safest Choice 46
Stepping Out of the Way 47
Regaining Your Balance 47
Are You Trapped or Free to Leave? 48
Ready Position 48
Setting Boundaries and Yelling for Help 48
The Cower Power Game 49
Practicing Self-Protection Techniques to Stay Safe From Threatening or Physically Aggressive Behavior 51

Chapter Eight
Getting Adults to Get Help **52**
Why Kids Don't Ask for Help 52
Tools for Getting Help 53
How You Ask for Help Matters 54
When to Wait and When to Interrupt 55
Be a Helpful Adult to Talk To 56
Adults Are the Ones In Charge 57
Teaching Young People How to Get the Attention of Busy Adults 58

Chapter Nine
Bully Physical Self-Defense Techniques **60**
Bully Tactics and Emergency-Only Tactics 60
Ask Your Adults 60
Pulling or Twisting Away to Escape 61
Bully Self-Defense Targets and Techniques 61
Success Stories 62
Preparing Young People to Use Bully Self-Defense Tactics 64

Chapter Ten
Coping With Shunning, Exclusion, and Gossip **65**
My Own Story 65
Relational Bullying 66

Kidpower is committed to respect for everyone, reaching out to people who are most vulnerable.

Adjusting Emotional Distance 67
The "I'd Like to Join the Game" Practice 68
The Meet-New-People Personal Safety Tactic 69
The Gossip Game 69
Compliments Practice 70
Addressing Relational Bullying and Providing Support 71

Chapter Eleven
Being Brave to Set Boundaries and Advocate for Others **72**
Setting Boundaries With Duck 72
Speaking Up About Putdowns 73
Walking Our Talk 75
Balance of Power 75
Speaking Up to Stop Prejudice 77
Preparing Young People to be Brave to Stop Bullying 80

Chapter Twelve
Peer Pressure Tactics **81**
Positive and Negative Peer Pressure and Triggers 81
Family Counselor and Author Sharon Scott 81
Using Tactics to Address Common Peer Problems 82
Preparing Young People to Deal With Peer Pressure 84

Chapter Thirteen
Preventing Sexual Harassment **85**
The Problem –AAUW Study 85
Harassment-Free Schools and Work Places 86
Addressing Sexism and Homophobia 87
Dealing With Unwanted Sexual Attention 88
Actions to Help Prevent and Stop Sexual Harassment of Young People 91

Chapter Fourteen
Other Solutions to Problems With Peers **92**
Double-Check for Assertiveness 92
Leave 92
Find Safe Friends 93
Know Your Choices 94
Write Things Down 96
Figuring out Different Solutions to Bullying Problems 97

Chapter Fifteen
Stopping Cyber-Bullying **98**
Being Hurtful with Greater Efficiency and Anonymity 98
Ensuring Responsible Use of Technology 99
Documenting and Reporting Cyber-Bullying Problems 100
Create a Written Communication Technology Safety Contract 101
Actions Adults Can Take to Help Prevent and Stop Cyber-Bullying 104

Chapter Sixteen
Practice as a Management Tool for Unsafe, Disrespectful Behavior **106**
"Let's practice making safer choices!" 106

Remember that Children Often Want to Do Something
   that Their Adults Think is a Bad Idea   107
Set a Good Example by Accepting and Managing
   Your Upset Feelings   107
Lecturing or Arguing Don't Help   107
Address Resistance with Creativity, Compassion, and Humor   108
Find Opportunities to Turn Problems into Practices   108
Practicing Solutions for Different Kinds of Behavior Concerns   109

Chapter Seventeen
Common Questions About Bullying

Common Questions About Bullying   **110**
How Will I Know if My Child Is Being Bullied?   110
What Should I Do if My Child Is Being Bullied at School?   110
What if My Child Is Bullying Other Kids?   114
Should I Say Anything to the Parents of a Child Who Is Bullying Mine?   117
What if My Child's Teacher Is Doing the Bullying?   118
How do I Teach Kids the Difference Between Someone Acting
  Friendly and Being a True Friend?   118

Chapter Eighteen
Building Strong "People Safety" Skills

Building Strong "People Safety" Skills   **121**
Assertive Advocacy   121
Teaching Children the Skill of Confidence   123
Teaching Children to Persist   125
The Power of Positive Practice   126
How to Pick a Good Self-Defense Program   128
How to Teach the Famous Kidpower Trashcan   130

Chapter Nineteen
Tools for Creating a United Front Against Bullying

Tools for Creating a United Front Against Bullying   **136**
Sample Bullying, Harassment, and Violence
   Prevention Proclamation   136
Sample School Action Plan   137
Sample School Policies   139
An Opportunity to Grow   140

Kidpower Safety Signs for Everyone, Everywhere   142

Other Resources From Kidpower   **148**
Workshops   148
Kidpower Website and Free On-Line Library   148
Kidpower Safety Comics for Older and Younger Children   148
Fullpower Safety Comics for Teens and Adults   149
Relationship Safety Book   149

An Invitation From Irene   150

Acknowledgements and Contact Information   153

Note from the Author

Dear Readers,

Bullying can happen to anyone, anywhere.

As a child, I was shunned and taunted for several years by a group of girls at my elementary school every recess, day after day after day. And, I am sorry to confess that sometimes I bullied my younger sister and brother, even though I have always dearly loved them, because I lacked the skills to solve problems with them in a safer way. Like many young people, I also lacked the skills to manage my behavior in response to my own feelings and personal challenges that actually had nothing to do with my siblings at all.

As we now enter our third decade of teaching safety skills, we at Kidpower have heard countless stories of children who feel alone, sad, and scared because of bullying. And, we have countless examples of how our program has prepared adults to empower and protect the young people in their lives.

The stories here are all based on true situations. However, most of them have the names and details changed to protect the privacy of our students. Except where we have permission, any resemblance to anyone is coincidental.

Kidpower would not exist without the passion and generosity of thousands of people. Thank you to our center directors, instructors, advisors, donors, volunteers, workshop organizers and hosts, partner schools and organizations, funders, and students for your tremendous commitment.

Thank you to our program co-founder Timothy Dunphy, founding board president Ellen Bass, and my dear husband and organizational co-founder Ed van der Zande - all of you were essential in getting us going and are still important to keeping us going.

Thank you to Erika Leonard and Ian Price for your help in bringing this e-book into being so quickly. And, thank you to each of our senior program leaders and board members for your insights, enthusiasm, and support.

Together, we are working towards our vision of creating cultures of caring, respect, and safety for everyone.

Irene

Irene van der Zande
Kidpower Executive Director/Co-Founder

Chapter One
Bad News and Good News About Bullying

People Safety Skills – simple techniques to help people keep themselves and others safe.

"Ever since I moved to my new school, no one wants to be my friend. I cry every morning before I leave home."

"The kids on our street all used to have fun together. After our family decided to home school, one girl kept calling us weird. The neighborhood kids are siding with her. They say, 'If you don't want to go to our school, we don't want to play with you.' "

"A boy made up a webpage on a social networking site, and the page is full of mean things about me. 500 people said they liked that page. My stomach gets upset every time I think about it, which is almost all of the time."

"My best friend took an embarrassing photo of me when I wasn't looking and sent it to everyone we know. When I told her this was not okay, she told everyone that I am a slut. I wish I could just disappear."

"I am horribly allergic to peanuts and have even had to go to the emergency room. A boy keeps chasing me at the park with his peanut butter sandwich, shouting, 'You're going to DIE! You're going to DIE!'"

"During PE and lunchtime when no adults are around, other kids bump into me, spit on me, trip me, and then laugh and say it was an 'accident.' When I try to get adults to help, they tell me to work it out myself."

Bullying is a destructive force in the lives of far too many children. It's a direct attack on the self-esteem and well-being of the person targeted. A person participating in bullying can develop socially destructive behavior as well as feelings of guilt. Whether you are the target, the perpetrator, or the observer, bullying creates an upsetting and distracting environment in which to live, play, work, and learn.

The purpose of this book is to describe how adults can use Kidpower "People Safety" solutions to address bullying. We use the term "People Safety" to mean what individuals can do to take charge of the emotional and physical safety of themselves and others. In other words, people being safe with people.

Water Safety does not only mean drowning prevention, but also how to enjoy being in the water. Fire Safety does not only mean burning prevention, but also how to use fire for cooking, warmth, and fun.

In the same spirit, successful practice of "People Safety" skills can prepare children, teens, and adults to:

• Protect themselves from most bullying, abuse, and other problems with people;
• Create positive peer interactions;
• Build healthy relationships;
• Act as an advocate for stopping the bullying of others; and
• Find socially positive ways to manage the impulses that might tempt them to bully someone else.

In recent years, tragic news stories about suicides and school violence resulting from bullying have raised awareness about the importance of addressing this issue. Although different kinds of programs have helped, the problem continues. A 2007 study by the U.S. National Center for Education Statistics found that almost a third of students ages 12-18 reported that they had been bullied in school.

The good news is that adults can take action and teach effective skills that will protect children from bullying.

• Children who have strong, positive relationships with their adults are less likely to be vulnerable to becoming bullies or being bullied. They are also more likely to seek adult help if they need it.

• Children who know how to stay calm, aware, and confident are less likely to be chosen as targets for bullying.

• Children who respond to bullying attempts by setting boundaries and speaking up for themselves – or by calmly leaving with awareness, calm and confidence and going to get help if necessary – are less likely to remain targets of the person bullying.

• Children who know how to be assertive instead of aggressive and how to communicate respectfully are less likely to act like bullies. Children who know how to be persistent in getting help from busy adults are more likely to know what to do if they see bullying behavior.

Bullying tends to occur in environments where children spend much of their time. It often takes place in the context of relationships that are important to the child. The repeated nature of bullying, the desire to be accepted, and hurt feelings can make using People Safety skills challenging. Children often need extra help to apply and adapt these skills to fit their specific situations.

Children who have strong, positive relationships with adults and good "people safety" skills are much less likely to be bullied.

Chapter Two
Some Facts About Bullying

Everyone has the right to feel safe.

According to Our Experts – What Our Students Tell Us
According to Ken Rigby, Ph.D.
What the Research Means for Caring Adults
Times Have Changed
How Do People Bully?
Ideas for Discussing Bullying with Children

Bugs Bunny. Bart Simpson. Harry Potter. Garfield and Odie. Daffy Duck. Huck Finn. Pinnocchio. Rudolph the Red Nosed Reindeer. Charlie Brown and Lucy. Dorothy, The Scarecrow, The Tin Man, the Cowardly Lion, and the Wicked Witch. The Ugly Duckling. Edward Scissorhands. Tweety Bird and Sylvester the Cat. Spiderman. Scrooge. Popeye and Brutus. Little Orphan Annie. Oliver Twist. Tom and Jerry. The Roadrunner and Wiley E. Coyote. Cinderella and her stepsisters. Jean Valjean from Les Miserable. Caliban from The Tempest. Asterix and Obelix. Calvin and Hobbs. The Karate Kid.

Some of the best-loved characters in books and film were bullied, bullied others, or both. Bullying used to be taken for granted as a normal part of childhood. Now, we know differently. So, what does bullying look like and why does this happen?

According to Our Experts – What Our Students Tell Us
Sometimes we ask children during a workshop, "What's bullying?" Hands shoot into the air and the answers pour out of our students. Because adults have more official words for the same behavior, I have put these in parentheses next to the explanations of our Kidpower experts:

- "When another kid tries to hurt or scare you." (Physical bullying; intimidation.)
- "When someone says bad stuff about you behind your back." (Relational bullying.)
- "When someone calls you names or makes fun of you." (Emotional abuse.)
- "When kids leave you out." (Shunning.)
- "When kids gang up on you and try to make you give them your money or your stuff." (Extortion.)
- "When someone copies you in a way that makes you look dumb." (Mimicking.)
- "When other people say or do things to bother you over and over on purpose." (Harassment.)
- "When someone tries to make you do something that will get you into trouble." (Coercion.)
- "When someone tries to use their power to make you feel bad." (Bullying.)

We then ask our students, "Have you ever been bullied or seen someone else being bullied?" Most of them nod their heads. "How did you feel?" we ask. Again, our young and wise Kidpower experts raise their hands and say:

- "Sad."
- "I thought there must be something wrong with me."
- "Scared and wanting to hide."
- "Embarrassed and like I never wanted to go back."
- "Mad and like I wanted to get back at them."
- "As if I was the only person in the world that this was happening to."
- "Guilty because I was glad it wasn't happening to me."
- "Worried because I was afraid it would happen to me."
- "Ashamed because I didn't know what to do to stop it."
- "Frustrated."
- "Lonely."
- "Like I wanted to throw up or disappear."

According to Ken Rigby, Ph.D.

Ken Rigby, who has a doctorate in psychology, was employed as a teacher for ten years in elementary and high schools in England and Australia before becoming a professor at the University of South Australia. He has been doing research on bullying since the early 1990s, has published educational materials that are used by schools worldwide, and is considered a leading international expert on the subject of school bullying.

According to Rigby, a generally accepted definition of bullying is a "repeated oppression, psychological or physical, of a less powerful person by a more powerful person or group of persons." He points out that bullying is different from aggression between people of equal power.

He also points out that a child might end up having less power than others in a specific peer group as a result of many different kinds of factors. Being shy, liking poetry instead of sports, having a problem at home, lacking confidence, looking different, having a disability, being of a different culture, or being small might take away some power in the eyes of a peer group. A child might get greater power in a peer group because of factors such as size, quick wits, charisma, good looks, sports skill, a sharp tongue, or social status.

In 1999, Rigby presented his research in a paper titled, "What Harm Does Bullying Do?" at the Children and Crime: Victims and Offenders Conference convened by the Australian Institute of Criminology. Based upon extensive surveys of more than 38,000 Australian school children, his study found that at least 50 percent of children reported being bullied at school and approximately one child in six reported being bullied at least weekly by another child or group of students.

The majority of these children reported that they felt angry or sad and felt worse about themselves afterwards. In some cases, the cycle continued for weeks, months, and even years.

In a related study reported in the same paper, Rigby found a correlation between illness and being bullied and stated that there is likelihood that

Bullying is not new. What is new is our awareness of the damage it causes.

approximately one of every ten children who have been bullied will suffer long-term mental or physical health problems. He also indicated that the stress of bullying would be likely to affect academic performance.

Rigby's findings continue to be confirmed by many other studies around the world. To take just one example, according to the National Education Association, in the United States alone, 160,000 children miss school each day due to fear of being tormented by their classmates.

Sadly, instead of feeling safe and happy, 50% of kids report being bullied at school..

What the Research Means for Caring Adults
Any search for "bullying" on the Internet will show extensive research citations with very similar results. Across many countries, income groups, and cultures, researchers have found that:

• Bullying occurs frequently.
• Bullying is likely to be upsetting and potentially damaging both to the person being bullied and to people witnessing the bullying.
• Being allowed to bully, although sometimes rewarding in the short run, is likely to be damaging to the people doing the bullying in the long run.
• Stopping bullying takes a united, sustained, and consistent commitment by a school's parents, teachers, administration, and students.

Times Have Changed
Bullying is not new. What is new is our awareness of the damage it causes. Just as smoking, which was once thought to be a harmless habit, is now recognized as a major health hazard, bullying is increasingly understood to be a dangerous social hazard. We are learning about the destructive results of behavior that used to be accepted as a normal fact of life.

When I was growing up, children were told that they needed to learn how to deal with bullying on their own. Typical advice included:

• "*Fight back.* Don't let anyone walk all over you. Give as good as you get." The problem with this advice is that teaching children to fight over insults or property can put them in danger. An aggressive response might solve the problem one day, but lead to an increased likelihood of facing retaliation another day. At Kidpower, we believe that there can be a time and a place to fight to stop bullying but that fighting should be taught as the *last* resort.

• "*Don't let it get to you. Just ignore it.*" Unfortunately, chronic aggression directed toward you or jokes at your expense are hard to ignore, especially in situations where you cannot just leave, such as in school or among family members.

• "*Go find another friend.*" The betrayal that comes with a friend turning into a bully can be devastating.

• "*You'll get over it.*" When I ask adults to tell their childhood memories about bullying, the stories and the pain often sound fresh, as if the bullying happened yesterday.

• "*It isn't the end of the world.*" When you have to see people every day who are turned against you, it can seem endless.

In addition to the research mentioned above, well-publicized tragedies have caused adults to take bullying far more seriously than they did in the past. Children have killed themselves – and others – because of bullying.

Most people don't die because of bullying. However, the effect of bullying is like the effect of pollution. Polluting chemicals in the environment don't usually kill people right away unless they get a strong dose, but even low-level exposure over time can undermine health   Continued exposure over time can increase the damaging effects. The same seems to be true with bullying.

How Do People Bully?

Different forms of bullying include:

- **Physical** – threatened or actual physical harm such as making intimidating threats, pushing, shoving, hitting, tripping, poking, kicking, or acting in a dominating way.

- **Emotional** – actions intended to make someone else feel uncomfortable such as name-calling, using put-downs, making insulting gestures, exchanging knowing looks, copying/mimicking, or making rude sounds.

- **Relational** – attacking someone's relationships with others through shunning, repeating destructive gossip, slandering, making embarrassing pictures public, back-stabbing, giving someone "the silent treatment," or sharing private information with others.

Any or all of these forms of bullying can be used to extort money or property or to pressure someone into acting in a way that is harmful or forbidden.

Parents have told us countless stories of their children being bullied in many imaginative and cruel ways that were often not understood by the adults around them. As Kim's mother said, "A girl in Kim's class was drawing cartoons that showed Kim getting into humiliating situations. This girl would get other kids to look and giggle, because the cartoons are very clever. Then, she'd 'accidentally' leave the cartoons for Kim to find. After this had gone on for months, Kim announced that she didn't want to go to school anymore."

Whether the form of delivery is to someone's face, through others, on the phone, in writing, in pictures, through texting, through social media, or through e-mail, everyone needs to understand that bullying is bullying and is ultimately damaging to everyone involved.

Ideas for Discussing Bullying with Children

1 Ask children leading questions such as, "What is bullying? Have you ever been bullied or seen bullying? How did you feel?"

2 Explain the different types of bullying and let children know that you think this is wrong.

3 Point out bullying behavior in stories, movies, or pictures. Ask what different choices each party might make - the one doing the bullying, the one being bullied, and anyone watching the bullying.

4 Tell children very specifically, "You and others have the right to be safe at home, at school, and everywhere you go. Bullying is unsafe. If you are being bullied or see someone being bullied, I want you to tell me. If you make a mistake and do something hurtful to someone, I also want to know so we can figure out how to fix the problem."

5 Have children draw pictures, write stories, or role play about bullying problems and solutions.

A fun, safe way for kids to use their power to affect the world around them.

Chapter Three

What Makes Bullying Hard to Stop?

Most Babies Come With Everything
Why Do People Bully?
Whether Behavior is Bullying or Leadership Can Depend on the Rules
But It's Just a Joke!
From the Mouths of "Innocents"
Victim Behavior
Prejudice
Poor Adult Role Models
Acceptance That This Is Just the Way Things Are
Peer Orientation
Ideas for Dealing with Issues That Make Bullying Hard to Stop

E ven with all of the media attention on tragic news stories, all of the millions of dollars spent on bullying prevention programs, and the tremendous efforts of countless concerned adults, bullying is not likely to disappear as a social problem anytime in the near future, if ever. One US study says that reported school bullying is less. Another says that school violence, including bullying, is vastly underreported. Why does bullying continue despite the best efforts of so many people?

Most Babies Come With Everything

Kids are born with the power to think, make noise, and move. Very quickly, they learn how to use this power to affect the world around them. As they grow, most children have the potential to be aggressive and passive, followers and leaders, cruel and kind... all of this is normal behavior.

At the same time, children come with different tendencies. They might have the tendency to:

• define themselves by pushing against boundaries until someone or something pushes back;
• get upset more easily than other children;
• give in or go along with others;
• wait and join the side that seems to be winning; or
• get worried and leave if a situation seems unsafe.

All of this is normal behavior.

If you watch a group of young children playing, they will often experiment with being bullies, being enthusiastic followers, and being disturbed witnesses – as well as with being unhappy victims. Sometimes they go back and forth between different roles quite quickly. In fact, the minute the power structure changes, bullies often become victims and victims often become bullies.

Part of what makes bullying hard to stop is that "might makes right" behavior is natural. Much of what we require children to do is necessary, but *not* natural. For the sake of functioning in a civilized society, we teach children to contain their natural impulses to grab food, knock others out of their way, look or touch anywhere their curiosity suggests, and use any place they wish as a toilet.

The way that children learn positive social skills is often by experimenting with negative ones and getting feedback from their adults and other children. Neither catastrophizing this experimentation nor letting it go will help children learn positive ways of interacting. On the one hand, I feel sad when I hear of stories such as the one about the five-year-old boy who was expelled from school for sexual assault because he lifted up the skirt of a little girl. On the other hand, I feel worried when I see adults letting children run wild in the name of not curtailing their natural impulses.

Why Do People Bully?

I believe that most of us are good people, but most of us will probably do something that others experience as bullying at some point in our lives. As a child, I occasionally bullied my younger sister and brother. I was supposed to be in charge of them, but I didn't know how. Mostly, I bullied them because I felt frustrated and overwhelmed. Also, I hate to admit this now, but sometimes I thought they were little brats, and they just annoyed me!

When I tell kids this, they giggle. I explain that I feel sorry about it now, but I didn't know better at the time. I then ask them, "Can you think of times when you bullied someone and why you did it?"

Given a safe space and permission, young people can be painfully honest in their replies:

• "I was bored and picking on her felt like fun."

• "I was scared some kids would get me so I got them first."

• "I wanted to feel important, and making him cry was a way to get people to look up to me."

• "I wanted something he had, so I took it."

• "She hurt my feelings, so I wanted to get even."

• "My mom and dad were always fighting at home, and I felt so angry and sad all the time. I wanted to hit something or yell at someone just to try to feel better. Something about yelling or hurting someone else made me feel like I was giving some of my pain away."

• "I thought it was just a joke and not that important."

"Something about yelling or hurting someone else made me feel like I was giving some of my pain away."

Experimenting with bullying behavior is normal, but as adults, our job is to help children make safer choices.

• "I was jealous, and she seemed so stuck up. I wanted to bring her down to size."

• "He was *so* pathetic and seemed to be just asking for it."

If a child is looking for attention, recognition, entertainment, distraction, or release of irritation, bullying can be an effective way to get what she or he wants, at least in the short run. Unless adults acknowledge this reality, figuring out how to provide positive alternatives along with the clear message that this destructive behavior is unacceptable will be difficult.

Whether Behavior is Bullying or Leadership Can Depend on the Rules

Part of what makes this issue confusing for young people is that behavior that is seen as bullying in one context can be necessary for success in another. People who are highly successful in fields such as sports, business, and politics are often shown in the popular media as being rewarded for what we would consider to be bullying behavior in another context. The rules for what is and is not acceptable are changing and vary in different societies.

My descriptions in this section reflect what young people are likely to see – and perhaps misunderstand – in the world of politics, business, and sports. These are not social or academic contexts; they are government and business environments. The participants usually make an informed, adult decision to be in these contexts, and they have the power to leave.

For example, the players in a professional basketball game are not in the same context as players in a children's school basketball game. The professional players have entered into an agreement with a major money-making business, and they are paid to play. The children may not even have a choice about playing in their game at all. Talking about these differences with kids can lead to interesting conversations and realizations for everyone.

In competitive sports, athletes often need to push physically and aggressively right up to the boundaries to win. However, if they go over the boundaries in the opinion of the referee, the team is penalized and the offending member might even lose the right to continue to play in the game.

Sometimes the popular media sends a message that business leaders have to be "bullies" in order to be successful. The reality is that success in highly competitive, fast moving markets often requires someone who can lead decisively and take calculated risks.

Taken too far, however, a corporate culture that rewards intimidation and bullying behavior can find itself engaging in unethical and even illegal behavior. In extreme cases like that of Enron, a major American energy company that went bankrupt after committing accounting fraud, a bullying culture can also lead to the financial collapse of a major company, the loss of jobs for thousands of workers, and felony convictions for corporate officers.

Behavior in politics can also look like bullying behavior. In the United States, negative campaigning or publicly criticizing an opponent seems to be part of every election cycle for both parties. Stretching the truth or even outright

   19

lying also seems to be tolerated up to a point to further a politician's agenda. However, there are checks and balances in terms of how much of this behavior is tolerated. If politicians say or do something that "goes too far" according to the changing court of "public opinion," they can lose elections or be forced to resign from their positions. And, someone who breaks the law is held accountable.

Children can understand that the rules are different in different situations. For everyone, acceptable behavior on a basketball court is just not the same as acceptable behavior in a living room, classroom, or store. Your conversations can help them develop an understanding that even acceptable behavior in professional basketball may not be the same as acceptable behavior in their local youth league games.

We need to be aware that our children may see many examples of aggressive or bullying-type behavior through the media and in their everyday lives. We need to be careful of our own behavior, remembering that we are important role models of our children. We can explain to children that though they may see examples of negative ways of handling situations, we have different expectations for their behavior. When children are younger, we can say, "Yes, I know that politicians sometimes say mean things about other people to win an election, but those are grown-ups in politics. We're talking about kids in school. It's against the rules to be mean to someone here in our school."

As children get older, we can teach them about values and how to find ways to be powerful and effective leaders without being bullies. Children also need to know that some people who feel pressured by them might use this label as a form of fighting back. Certainly, I have been called a "bully" when I have had to set boundaries with others, even though I do my best to be respectful and fair in all my interactions with people.

But It's Just a Joke!
Unfortunately, our society teaches children that being rude and unkind is cool and funny. Through the media, children identify with characters in cartoons, movies, and shows. These characters are often showing children countless examples of saying and doing hurtful things to each other as a joke.

Sometimes children don't understand the difference between reality and pretend. After watching a movie that showed people pulling off each other's pants as a joke, a little boy got into trouble because he tried to do the same thing at school. He was confused because his parents had laughed at the man in the movie but were upset with him.

Even more often, kids – and adults, too – don't know the difference between funny jokes and hurtful teasing. Funny jokes can be about what someone is good at or doesn't mind being bad at. If everyone involved or being joked about would agree that it's funny, then a joke is funny. If they would not all agree, then it's hurtful, not funny.

As child psychologist and entertainer Peter Alsop says, "Before I tell a joke about green Martians with four eyes, I go ask some of my four-eyed green Martian friends what they think of the joke. If they don't think it's funny, then

Unfortunately, our society teaches children that being rude and unkind is cool and funny.

I can learn something about them I need to know. And if they think it's funny, then I feel fine telling it to a whole roomful of four-eyed green Martians!"

Hurtful teasing usually means making fun of the ways someone has trouble doing something or putting someone down for being different. It's just as important to stop hurtful teasing as it is to stop hurtful hitting.

What seems like a joke to one person can be devastating to another. As one successful professional woman told me, "My childhood was a misery because the other kids made fun of me for being fat. Years later, I found myself in therapy dealing with the pain caused by their laughter."

Even if some children are protected from developing the "being-mean-is-funny" belief in their homes, just one child in a group can affect the dynamic of a group, leading to a behavior epidemic of many of the children saying hurtful things to get their way, to be cool, to be funny, and to try to keep themselves from being targeted.

From the Mouths of "Innocents"

Finding out what children actually say to each other can be eye opening. A teacher once asked me to come to her third grade classroom because the teasing had gotten completely out of hand. Of course, the teacher stopped the children when she heard them, but she couldn't be everywhere all the time. She wanted her students to stop themselves.

I started by asking the children, "Well, what is it that you're saying to each other?"

They looked at their teacher to see if answering me was okay. No adult had asked them this question so bluntly before. Then the words came pouring out. Both the teacher and I were shocked. It was quickly obvious that this was not language that could be said out loud in an adult's presence in any school without parental permission. Instead, we had the children write the words down.

I still have a file with their misspelled words on smudged, torn scraps of paper in childish printing. Curse words. Toilet words. Swear words. Graphic sexual language. Terribly threatening words. Words attacking race, religion, gender, sexual orientation, body size, and body parts. All from bright, innocent eight-year-olds!

What had started as a game between a few children because of annoyance or boredom had grown into a destructive culture involving the whole classroom. By taking the time to address the issue and to help her children understand the consequences of their language, the teacher turned a bad situation into a positive learning experience.

Victim Behavior

In addressing bullying issues, be aware that perfectly confident, competent children can be selected as targets for bullying for reasons that have nothing to do with their behavior. If they don't get help, these children might start showing victim behavior – or start acting like bullies themselves.

No one deserves to be bullied. However, some behaviors make it more likely for a child to be chosen as a target for bullying. Other kids are more likely to pick on someone who is acting weak or limp. Many kids are also likely to pull away and distance themselves if someone approaches them sounding hopeless, whiny, or helpless.

I have had kids, and adults too, ask me in frustration, "What if the person *deserves* it?"

I tell them, "You can set boundaries with someone without being mean."

However, if you are dealing with someone who seems to be submissive but whose actions are actually quite negative, this is called passive-aggressive behavior, and it can make boundary setting difficult.

Just as some children have learned to get attention by acting like bullies, other children have learned to get attention by acting like victims. Children who do not feel powerful might try to get their way through passive-aggressive behavior, which can be annoying to adults and infuriating to their peers. The feeling about such children is often that they are just "asking for it."

The truth, of course, is that they are not "asking for" a negative reaction from others, but they might be provoking it. With both children and adults, passive-aggressive behavior includes:

- Sabotaging activities and relationships though delaying, forgetting, not following through, or losing or breaking things by accident;
- Not being clear about what they do or don't want, so that they say, "Yes" and mean "No" or give mixed signals;
- Going along with people in positions of authority or who they perceive to have more power rather than standing up for themselves or their friends;
- Constantly whining and complaining, with never a good word to say about anybody;
- Lying or exaggerating to get others in trouble; and/or
- Acting put-upon and blaming others for everything that goes wrong rather than taking responsibility.

Adults can help children change passive-aggressive or other victim behavior. When children learn how to communicate assertively, they are more likely to get what they want. They can practice sounding and acting aware, calm, and confident, no matter how they feel inside.

Prejudice
Teasing is a common form of bullying and often gets dismissed as a natural result of differences. According to cross-cultural communications trainer Lillian Roybal Rose, "Differences by themselves are never the true problem. What causes the problem is that someone feels a need to dominate others in order to feel good about himself or herself. Unless individuals feel worthy and whole within themselves, they are likely to try to dominate others or to accept domination from others in ways that are hurtful."

Discomfort or curiosity are different from bullying. We need to accept that

*No one deserves to be bullied, **but** some behaviors make it more likely for a child to be chosen as a target for bullying.*

for many people, feeling uncomfortable if something or someone seems different from what they are used to is natural. In fact, being wary of what is unfamiliar is important survival behavior. However, part of successful evolution for any species also includes the ability to adapt to new situations and to learn what differences are dangerous and what differences are interesting or even useful.

Children are not wrong to notice and comment on different ways that people look, speak, act, dress, and eat. The problem comes when their adults encourage or allow them to do this in ways that are unkind or that lump together people who might share one characteristic into a larger category combining many characteristics.

Children can learn how to be interested and curious without being rude. It's normal but potentially hurtful for children to shout at the kindergarten lunch table, "Eeeu. Why's she eating that weird stuff with those little sticks?" This reaction can become bullying when it turns into repeated chronic putdowns. Instead, children can learn to ask respectful questions, such as, "What's that? What does it taste like? Will you tell me about the sticks you are using?"

Prejudice grows when adults serve as models, making negative assumptions and thoughtless remarks overheard by children, like, "The crime rate is rising because so many of *those* people are moving into our neighborhood." Or, "Poor thing. He can't help it. His parents are getting divorced." Prejudice grows when adults make or laugh at jokes that are racist, sexist, homophobic, or otherwise negatively stereotype a group of people.

All of it is a form of prejudice – the assumption that people who are different from the majority group or the group with the most perceived power in some way are less worthy than people who are not. Differences might have to do with income, race, culture, martial status, disability, religion, sexual orientation or identity, politics, age, health, mental health, family situations, education, etc. Unless someone's behavior is directly destructive to another person, these differences are not reasons to be aggressive, even if people might strongly disagree about some of them.

Adults can create environments in schools, families, and communities that celebrate diversity and that identify and refuse to accept prejudiced remarks or behavior. Many schools are doing a great job of building understanding by teaching children about different cultures, reading books about different kinds of abilities and different kinds of families, and letting children know about the contributions to our society of people from many different backgrounds. As children get older, they can learn how to become informed consumers of the media and about how prejudice is created and perpetuated in ways that lead to violence and abuse.

Poor Adult Role Models

Being rude and belligerent to get your way is often directly modeled for children by responsible adults. Shortly after my husband first came to the United States from the Netherlands, we attended a school board meeting where people had strong disagreements with each other. Many parents had brought their children to put pressure on the school board.

> *Prejudice grows when adults make or laugh at jokes that are racist, sexist, homophobic, or otherwise negatively stereotype a group of people.*

Ed was appalled at the threatening remarks and rude behavior, especially in front of children, by people on all sides of the conflict – parents, teachers, principals, and school board members. I remember him asking me in an astonished voice, "Are we still in the Wild West here?"

Even though most of the teachers and other adults in my childhood were wonderful people, I remember a few teachers, camp counselors, and youth group leaders who were terrible role models. They put children down, played favorites, spread gossip, and made threatening remarks.

I have often had teachers or principals tell me of their frustration when parents spread gossip about students or families at the school, sometimes in person and sometimes by e-mail. Spreading gossip that undermines someone's reputation is a form of bullying. It would have been far better modeling for those parents to go directly to the adult in charge – the principal or the teacher – to discuss their concerns.

Again, having an interest in what is happening to others is normal. People who slow down when they see an accident on the other side of the road are not evil. Some might just want to understand what's going on. Some might want to see if anyone needs help. However, people who block the road to look at an accident or even to take pictures are being destructive.

The same thing is true with gossip. Concern or curiosity about what is happening in one's neighborhood, family, or school is normal. However, repeating gossip that damages someone's reputation without a very good reason is destructive. The desire to retaliate, punish, 'give them what they deserve', or 'bring someone down a notch' does not count as a good reason.

If adults want children to stop bullying, we need to set an example by not acting like bullies or victims ourselves. Children need to see adults modeling being powerful, respectful leaders. If we notice when we are engaging in destructive behavior towards others, we can set a good example by stopping ourselves and apologizing.

Acceptance That This Is Just the Way Things Are

On the first day of school after summer vacation, my son Arend at age nine came home and said, "I had a hard day, Mommy. My shell got soft over the summer." "What shell do you mean?" I asked him.

"The shell that keeps out the mean things that people say and do to each other," Arend explained. "Without my shell, everything bothered me." My son looked at my troubled face and added, "Don't worry, Mommy. My shell will harden soon."

Arend was in a school that he loved. I was sad that, even in this caring place, my child's perception was that he needed to harden his emotional shell in order not to be upset by the behavior of others.

The reality is that, as hard as I try, I have yet to find a place where children are always kind and thoughtful to each other. We can enforce a respectful environment in the short-term context of a Kidpower class, but in a longer-

Children need strong adult attachment.

term relationship, people get on each other's nerves, say or do things that someone will experience as hurtful, or cross each other's boundaries.

The reality is that, when people have different perspectives and interests, they are likely to have problems. What is important is that we make a continued commitment to keep working things out in ways that are respectful instead of becoming apathetic and accepting that "this is just the way things are." Unlike adults, most children do not have the choice of leaving their family, school, or neighborhood. This means that their adults need to keep working to teach children how to relate to each other respectfully and also to create positive relationships in all aspects of their lives.

Peer Orientation

In their wise and compelling book, *Hold On To Your Kids*, authors Gordon Neufeld, Ph.D., and Gabor Mate, M.D., explain how children's attachment to peers over parents leads to a host of social ills, including bullying. They make a strong case for the importance of parents and other adults seeing their relationships with their children as their top priority, even during the teen years when it can seem normal for young people to pull away.

Neufeld and Gabor point out that children need a strong attachment with a primary "source of authority, contact, and warmth" in order to thrive. If they do not have this with their parents or other consistent adult caregivers, children are likely to end up becoming oriented towards their peers instead. In our society, children are often seduced into peer attachments at the expense of parental and other adult attachments through a lack of parental time, through peer-oriented school cultures, and through technology such as text messages and e-mail.

Peer orientation can lead to children dominating others, to children accepting destructive behavior towards themselves in order to be accepted, and to children participating in hurtful actions – all in order to meet their attachment needs.

The authors explain that children are more likely to learn and to accept boundaries from adults in the context of a strong, positive relationship, rather than by quick fix parenting strategies. *Hold On To Your Kids* includes excellent ideas for parents and other adults on how to create, sustain, and regain attachments with their children.

Ideas for Dealing with Issues That Make Bullying Hard to Stop

1 Make having a positive, connected relationship with the children in your life your top priority. If children seem to be pulling away, keep reaching out to them. If you get stuck in a negative dynamic with your children, don't just accept this as inevitable. Try to find ways to reconnect. If need be, get professional help.

2 Make bullying against the rules of your family, school, and community groups. Address the causes of bullying and what makes it hard to stop that might be true for the children in your care.

3 Discuss bullying with children by asking questions and listening to their answers. Useful questions include: What is bullying? Have you ever been bullied? What happened? What can you do to protect yourself? Have you ever seen bullying? What happened? What can you do if you see someone being bullied? Have you ever bullied someone else? What happened? What can you do to stop yourself from acting like a bully?

4 Make sure that adults are setting an excellent example for children. Don't let people bully you. Make sure that you are not bullying others. Have adults learn and model skills for communicating concerns assertively and setting boundaries effectively and respectfully with each other as well as with children

5 Teach children conflict resolution skills and have a structure that supports their getting adult help when this doesn't work. Children often need help to re-state concerns or discuss issues in ways that are respectful.

6 Notice bullying behavior and address it immediately. Make the consequence of bullying behavior be to rehearse behaving in a respectful way. If a child is pushing against boundaries, have that child practice how to feel one way and act another. When a child is acting like a victim, have that child practice acting assertively instead. When children start being mean to each other, intervene by changing the context or by saying, "That (be specific about the behavior) looks unsafe to me. Please be in charge of your words and body."

7 Keep paying attention to ensure that children stay respectful when you are not directly supervising.

8 Try to give children a media diet that includes positive role models as well as poor ones. Point out poor role models shown to children and say, "That looks like bullying, doesn't it? What would be a more respectful and safer way of handling this situation?"

9 Model empathy and respect for differences. Look for programs that teach children about cross-cultural communication. Expose them to stories, examples, and media presentation that show why it is important to value people for their differences as well as the ways that they are the same.

Talking to someone you trust can help.

Chapter Four

Managing Emotional Triggers to Prevent Explosions

Emotional Safety Techniques to Deal With Bullying
Get Specific
Taking the Power Out of the Word "Crybaby"
Reframing the Word "Bitch"
The "Asshole" Success Story
But What if We Both Like It?
Staying in Charge of Your Body and Your Words
Teaching Children to Manage Their Emotional Triggers

At any age, bullying can create a vicious cycle of people pushing each other's emotional hot buttons or triggers. People who bully often justify their behavior because they believe that they have been bothered or offended by the ones they are bullying. Instead of handling these feelings in a safe fashion and being stopped if they don't, they say and do hurtful things. People who get bullied often respond by getting triggered in such a way that they might seem like ones who are causing the problem, because they act visibly angry or whiny instead of responding with a firm boundary and by seeking help.

Emotional Safety Techniques to Deal With Bullying
Have you ever replayed someone's cruel or thoughtless words or behavior towards you over and over in your mind, feeling miserable every time the picture of what happened pops into your thoughts? Children and youth do that too. Often their hurt and angry feelings will grow over time, instead of fading, especially if the bullying behavior becomes chronic so that they are forced to deal with it constantly.

A big part of emotional safety for people of any age is recognizing and taking the power out of your emotional triggers. Emotional triggers are thoughts, words, or gestures that cause people to explode with feelings. People can explode in different ways including:

• Getting sad and hurt;
• Freezing;
• Getting angry;
• Acting frantic.
• Trying urgently to please someone or be noticed by someone.

Learning to manage personal triggers can be a huge help in stopping bullying.

Kidpower teaches several emotional safety techniques to protect yourself from being triggered by hurtful words and behavior. The following techniques have worked for children as young as 2 and for adults as old as 102.

Using your arm to make a trash can to throw away hurting words.

- **Getting Centered, or 'Calm Down Power'.** Push your palms together. Take a breath. Straighten Your Back. Feel where your feet are. Focus on something peaceful.

- **The Kidpower Trash Can.** Take one hand and put it on your hip. The hole your arm makes is your Kidpower Trash Can. Use your other hand to catch hurting words before they get into your heart or your head, where they can stay stuck for a really long time. Now, throw the hurting into your Trash Can. Now, put your hand and your heart and say something nice to yourself. You can do this in your imagination or with a real trash can. You can do this with hurtful words others say or that you say to yourself.

For a detailed explanation, see the section on How to Teach the Famous Kidpower Trash Can on pages 130-143.

- **The Screen.** Imagine a screen protecting you from the other person, keeping out insults and letting in useful information - like the screen on a window keeps out the bugs and lets in fresh air.

- **The Emotional Raincoat.** If someone is storming and you cannot just leave, imagine that you are in a real storm, wearing a warm, waterproof raincoat. You can be silent or make non-escalatory statements like, "I am sorry you feel that way. I care about you a lot. We see this differently. We can agree to disagree. You are important to me."

- **'That's Not True' Practice.** Sometimes people say something about you that is true and mix it with something that is not. For example, someone might say, "You're awful because you're different." Even if it is true that you are different than others, this does not mean you are awful. Make a fence by putting your hands in front of your heart a little away from your body, palms facing outwards. Practice by having someone say true things mixed up with untrue things. Use your fence to block the hurting words and say out loud, "That's not true!"

Get Specific

The first step in figuring out what the emotional triggers are is to ask children for specifics about *exactly* what others are saying or doing that is upsetting to them. General language such as "things we're not supposed to say" is not as useful as the specific words.

What is upsetting will be different for different people. For a younger child, the word "crybaby" can be as triggering as the worst foul language that you can imagine for teens or adults.

If we give words so much power that children cannot say them even to explain what's bothering them, then we are being unreasonable if we expect them not to be bothered. The most effective way to take the power out of really foul language is to let children say the words aloud, write them down, and practice not getting hurt or triggered when someone says these words to them.

The same thing is true with intimidating or rude gestures, sounds, or facial expressions. Children often speak in generalities because they don't want to sound silly or because the idea upsets them.

Language like "She keeps bothering me" is not as useful as "She glares every time I walk close by." Or, "She whispers and nudges my other friends as soon as I come over to talk to them." Or, "Every time I am next to her, she acts like she is going to knock me down or hit me." Encourage children to tell you the specifics so that you have a clear picture of what is going on and can help them make a plan for protecting themselves.

Taking the Power Out of the Word "Crybaby"

In a kindergarten classroom workshop, a five-year-old boy I'll call Craig did not want to try the trash can practice. To use the Trash Can Technique, students take words that hurt them and pretend to throw the words into a real or imaginary trash can instead of taking these words to heart.

Up until the name-calling part of the workshop, Craig had been enthusiastic. While the other kids were busy practicing with adult volunteers and teachers leading their little groups, I took Craig aside and we sat next to each other on the floor.

"Some mean words won't fit into your trash can," I told Craig, and then asked in a very matter-of-fact voice, "Is someone calling you names?"

"My big brothers call me 'crybaby' *every single day*!" Craig mumbled, with set wooden look.

"Oh, *my*!" I said. "That sounds upsetting. Can you think of a place besides the trash can to throw away the word 'crybaby'?"

"I want to throw it into my brother's mouth and sew his mouth shut!" Craig said firmly.

"Can you think of another place to throw this hurting word that is not attached to a person?"

"Well, I *could* cut off someone's butt and throw the word in there!" Craig looked as if this idea really appealed to him.

"It sounds to me as if you are *really* mad at your brothers!" I said sympathetically, reflecting that the teasing in Craig's home must have gotten pretty intense.

"*Yes*!" Craig muttered, glowering balefully.

"The problem with throwing mean words into someone else is that the meanness grows and gets bigger," I explained. "So can you think of something to do with the word 'crybaby' that will not go into any part of someone else, either attached or unattached?"

Craig thought for a few seconds while I waited quietly. "Maybe," he said. "I could shrink it and melt it away in some very hot sand!"

"This sounds like a very good plan!" I told him.

Later, in the whole group, without focusing on Craig, I explained to everyone that sometimes the Trash Can technique works but not always. If one thing doesn't work, you can always try something else. Sometimes people make fun of you for something that *is* true. Suppose someone makes fun of me because I have curly hair and says in a nasty voice or with a scrunched up face, "Eeeu! Your hair is *curly*!"

Suppose that I answer, "My hair is *straight*!" No one will believe me because my hair *is* curly. I can throw away the hurtful way they are talking about my hair into my trash can and say to myself, "I like my curly hair!"

If that doesn't work, I can think about what they are actually saying when they make fun of my hair, which is that there is something wrong with me because my hair is curly. After listening to people make fun of my curly hair, I might even start to say to myself, "I am *ugly* because my hair is curly!" But I can decide that that's not true.

I then told the class, "Let's all make a fence with our hands. Put your arms in front of you like this and push your hands away from you, like a fence. Now say, '*That's not true*!'"

They did and I explained, "What we are saying 'that's not true' to is not my curly hair, because that IS true, but to the mean way someone talks about it. Let's try out this idea with some other examples. Suppose a friend tells you in an upset voice, 'You are being a bad friend!' but what he or she is actually saying is, 'You are a bad friend because you want to play a different game than I do! Make your fence and say, '*That's not true*!'"

They did and I explained, "What you are saying 'that's not true' to is that you are a bad friend." Picking another example, I said, "If someone calls you, "dummy," what they actually are saying might be, 'You are dumb because you made a mistake!' And what do you say?"

Everyone stretched out his or her fences and said, "That's not true."

"What about 'You are a bad person because I am mad at you,'" I ask.

Again, everyone, adults and kids said, "*That's not true*!"

I reminded the class that having somebody mad at you *might* be true, but that it is not true that you are a bad person just because someone else is mad at you.

Having established the idea, I continued, "Sometimes people make fun of us because we cry. Who here has ever been called a 'crybaby'?" As we all, along

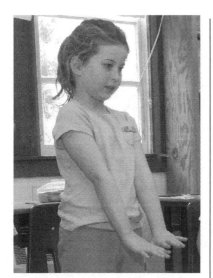

Making a fence to protect your feelings.

with Craig, looked around the room, almost everybody, including the adults, raised their hands.

I asked, "Did being called a crybaby hurt your feelings?" We all nodded, and I continued, "What it means if someone calls you a crybaby is that you are a baby if you cry, and that's not true!"

To give more information, I added a leading question, "Why do people cry??" I paused so the children could call out answers. "When they are sad," they said, "or mad."

"That's right!" I said. "Tears can come out of our eyes when we have upset feelings. And crying can be an safe way of getting upset feelings out of our bodies."

The class of five-year-olds was extremely interested and their parents and teachers were riveted, so I kept going, deliberately picking a story that had an older boy in it to reinforce the idea that even big boys cry. "Last year, I had a class with kids older than you and there was a boy we'll call Jim who was having a hard day and crying. Jim was embarrassed about crying and that made him cry harder. Has that ever happened to you?"

Most hands, including Craig's, were raised. "Anyway," I continued, "After I explained about tears and how crying can help our bodies be safe by getting rid of upset feelings, one of Jim's friends asked, 'Does that mean that when Jim cries, he is doing Kidpower?' Of course, Jim's friend was right because Kidpower helps keep you safe, and so can crying."

I smiled at my students and said, "If someone says, 'You are a baby because you cry' or calls you 'crybaby' for short, then even if you *are* crying, what do *you* say?"

Everyone made a fence with their hands and shouted, "*That's not true!*"

Because written words have extra power, we then wrote the word "*crybaby*" on a big piece of paper and made a drawing of a crying face. I held up the sign, and the kids immediately read or at least guessed the word. We passed the sign around, and each person tore part of the paper away. Finally, we all cheered while Craig crumpled the tattered pieces of the word *crybaby* and threw them into the real recycling bin nearby.

Reframing the Word "Bitch"

In researching definitions for the word "bitch," I felt that Wikipedia had the most comprehensive explanation of the different ways this word is used: "A 'bitch' is a female dog or other member of the canidae family. In colloquial use, the word bitch is often employed insultingly to describe a woman as malicious, spiteful, domineering, intrusive, unpleasant, or sexually promiscuous; it may also be used to refer to a male subordinate to another male (especially in prison to show domination over another). A bitch can also refer to somebody, usually a woman, who is mean or inconsiderate."

I have seen girls torment themselves endlessly over being called a bitch. "Am

I a bitch?" they worry. Or they get furious and rage, "How dare she call me a bitch! I'm not going to let her get away with this!"

In one workshop, I was teaching a group of girls who had gotten into trouble with the law to help them learn to control their power. Words and name-calling had triggered most of their fights. In their group home, they used this saying for reframing the word: "A bitch is a female dog. Dogs bark. Bark grows on trees and trees are part of nature and nature is *beautiful* so thank you for calling me a bitch!"

Even though they understood this idea, these girls still needed to *practice* staying calm and walking away instead of getting upset in order not to get into fights. We made a plan with the staff in their group home that having to practice how to make safer choices would be a natural consequence of fighting. Instead of giving lectures about fighting, the staff would have the girls re-state their feelings in non-attacking ways and walk away from insults. Later, we heard that the violence in their group home reduced dramatically.

Sometimes girls find words to go with the letters to reframe the word "bitch," such as:

B–beautiful, **I**–intelligent, **T**–talented, **C**–confident, **H**–happy.

Sometimes, with full permission of teachers and parents, we have whole rooms full of preteen and teen girls all shouting joyously a negative word – BITCH! – and then a positive word, such as their favorite food – PIZZA! The novelty of being given permission to say a swear word – because when else has a teacher asked them to do something like this? – does not take away from the lesson that a set of sounds does not need to make them miserable.

The "Asshole" Success Story

In the beginning days of Kidpower, Timothy and I were asked to conduct a private lesson with an eleven-year-old boy called Jeremy. Jeremy lived permanently in a group home because he had been abused so badly. He was targeted for relentless bullying by the other kids because he often lost control of his bowels.

Jeremy walked into the room so bent over that he looked as if he was in a fetal position. His head was down and he refused to make any eye contact. "So," I asked him, "What hurtful things do kids say to you?"

"I can't tell you," Jeremy whispered. "It's a bad word."

"You have permission from your counselors to tell us the word, even if you aren't supposed to say it." I explained.

With his head completely hidden, Jeremy whispered, "Asshole."

"Well then," I announced loudly. "We are going to take the power out of the word *asshole*!"

Jeremy looked shocked and sat down. At first, he was too upset to practice

Reframing negative words can help increase self-esteem.

with us, so Timothy modeled for him what to do.

"YOU DUMB ASSHOLE!" I shouted at Timothy. "YOU SHOULD BE ASHAMED! YOU ARE ALWAYS MESSING UP!"
Timothy took a big breath to get centered and then threw the hurting words away, saying, "I am proud of who I am."

Jeremy looked up at Timothy with big eyes and asked, "Do you really think I can do that?"

"It might be hard at first," Timothy explained. "But you have the right to protect your feelings and to feel good about yourself. It gets easier when you practice."

Over and over, Jeremy practiced with Timothy – getting centered, throwing away the hurting words, and saying good things to himself to take inside. He then went on to practice all the self-protection and self-defense skills. He left the room smiling, looking directly at us, and with his head held high.

A few weeks later we got a call from the director of the group home saying that Jeremy was doing great and that *all* of the bullying had stopped completely

But What if We Both Like It?
Sometimes when I stop behavior that looks like bullying to me, both children will protest, "But this is *fun*! I like it."

The reality is that sometimes in friendships, people do use insults as a way to reinforce their special relationship to each other. In fact, in some cultures, ritualized insults are used as a way of releasing tension and building community. The Dutch and the Belgians both make fun of each other's potato-eating habits without anyone being devastated or going to war.

This kind of playing can truly be a form of endearment rather than bullying *if*:

• The insults and dominating play are equal in power and go both ways.
• This kind of joking is hurting neither party. In other words, everyone involved understands that the intention of the joking is positive rather than to be hurtful.
• The joking hurts no bystanders and the joking is not directed towards damaging the credibility of other people.

The problem is that, too often, kids will persuade themselves that putdowns or being shoved around is okay with them because they want to be accepted and included. They don't want to lose the relationship, and they do want to seem cool. Rude, dominating behavior might actually feel okay in the moment because it is familiar and is better than the alternative, which is to be left out.

One-sided insults and dominating behavior are actually a way of reinforcing a power imbalance. If one person is doing the insulting and the other is going along with it in order to be accepted, this can be damaging over the long run.

Too often, kids will persuade themselves that bullying behavior is okay with them because they want to be accepted or included.

I tell children who want to tease in this way, "This behavior is distracting right now, even if it is okay with both of you." Children need to learn that behavior in public settings is often different from acceptable behavior in private settings.

If this is an engrained way of interacting, I ask young people to think about it. "Is one person dishing it out and the other person taking it? Does joking in this way cause you to think less of someone else?"

Finally, we always remind adults to remember that, no matter how kids feel about a game, one of the Kidpower boundary rules is that behaviors and activities need to be allowed by the adults in charge. If a behavior is not acceptable to the adult in charge, the adult can say that the behavior is not allowed, and the kids should be expected to stop for this reason alone.

Staying in Charge of Your Body and Your Words

The purpose of managing triggers is to be able to manage yourself. Our instructor John tells his students, "It is important to know that all of your feelings are normal and to be able to talk with an adult you trust whenever anything bothers you. Sometimes, though, it is safer to let yourself feel one way but act in a different way. No matter how you feel, your job is to stay in charge of your body and your words. For example, how many of you sometimes feel like yelling or hitting, but you stop yourself?"

John raises his hand and looks at some students raising their hands. "You do this to avoid trouble, right?" As his students' heads nod, John says, "So let's practice feeling one way and acting differently."

With younger children, he uses a silly example. "Right now, I want all of you to look at my nose and think about how funny it looks. Pretend that you feel like laughing at my silly nose. Don't say anything. Just think. Great. Right now, you are feeling one way and acting another! You can use this technique when you are scared by acting as if you are not scared. You can use it when you are mad by acting as if you are not mad."

With older children, John gets right to the point, acting out what he is saying and coaching his students to copy him. "Everybody hold up your hand as if you are so upset that you want to hit someone. Now take a big breath and lower your hands. Everybody flinch as if you are afraid. Now take a big breath and make your bodies strong. Excellent."

Suddenly, one of John's students says, "In real life, this is hard."
"Yes it is," John agrees. "That's why we practice."

As adults, it is our responsibility to help children stop destructive play or teasing.

Teaching Children to Manage Their Emotional Triggers

1 For older children, explain what triggers are and, as appropriate, how to identify and protect themselves from different kinds of emotional attacks

2 If a child is obsessing about things that others have said or done, ask for specifics. Discuss the words, the behaviors, and why they are so upsetting.

3 Explain that we do not have the power to control what other people say or do, but we can learn to use our power to control our reactions. Practice techniques such as the Trash Can, the Screen, and That's Not True to take the power out of the actual upsetting words or offensive behavior that the child finds upsetting

4 If the behavior involves inappropriate, threatening, or abusive touch, practice being about to do the behavior and being stopped before it actually happens with strong boundary-setting skills. In other words, don't actually touch the child in an inappropriate, threatening, or abusive way. If the child gets stuck, pause and coach the child so that she or he can be successful in protecting her/himself.

5 Have the child show you the bullying behavior while you use boundary-setting techniques and then reverse roles. Remember to coach children so that they are successful each step of the way.

6 Ask children to tell you about times when they have felt upset but stayed in charge of their bodies and words. Demonstrate and practice different ways of doing this.

Chapter Five

Target Denial to Avoid Trouble

Practicing walking with awareness, calm, and confidence.

What is Target Denial?
Noticing Potential Trouble
Don't Be There
The Have-a-Nice-Day! Self-Defense Tactic
What Most Mothers Prefer
Walking Past Trouble
The Fallacy of "Giving As Good As You Get"
Practicing Using Target Denial to Prevent Bullying

Knowing when and how to leave a difficult or dangerous situation is one of the most powerful self-protection tools we have. Unfortunately, kids hear a lot of negative labels about someone who chooses to leave a confrontation. They don't want to be seen as weak, wimpy, being a quitter, giving up, or not being tough enough to take it. Sadly, as children get older, the belief that they need to have the last word or fight back to be powerful can lead to their getting injured or killed. Not only can target denial help protect kids from bullying, but it can prepare young people to disengage from potential violence.

What is Target Denial?
We tell our students, "There is a secret martial arts technique handed down from martial artist to martial artist through the ages. It is the best technique of all time. It's called, 'Target Denial', which means denying yourself as a target. You could also call it, 'don't be there!'"

Our students practice how to Stay Aware, Calm, and Confident so that they will notice a problem and not be as likely to attract a potential bully. They learn to Move Away from potential trouble and how to use their Walk Away Power to be safe.

Noticing Potential Trouble
Instructors Liam and Jennifer show students how using their awareness can help them notice when someone's behavior is changing from safe to unsafe. They pretend to be two children who are standing next to each other in line, shoulder to shoulder, watching a game and waiting to play.

Liam asks, "Can we use our awareness and notice each other without staring right at each other?"

"Yes!" the students realize.

Jennifer gradually makes a few changes in her posture and facial expression at this point. She glares, clenches her jaw, and furrows her brow. She crosses her arms and makes all the muscles in her upper body tight. She moves her feet a step apart and takes a more aggressive stance.

Liam asks the students, "What can you notice with your awareness that makes you think, 'Hmmm, trouble might be on the way over where Jennifer is standing.....'"

Even Kindergarteners are able to identify these changes easily and confidently. "I notice her eyes," one might say. "The way her arms are pulled in and tight," another will notice. "The way she's standing," says another.

Often, a child will say, "She looks angry." Liam will agree and then add more information: "Yes, it does look like she might be angry. But, is it also possible she has a stomach ache and is looking into the sun?" The students murmur agreement that this could be true.

"We can use our awareness to notice changes in people's behavior. But, that doesn't mean we know for sure what someone is feeling, thinking, or planning to do."

On an everyday basis, adults can help young people build this skill of noticing the difference between observations – "she is crossing her arms and glaring" – and conclusions – "she is angry." Their conclusions might be correct, but the ability to distinguish between the two helps people make decisions more effectively.

Liam says, "Right now, I'm not going to worry about what Jennifer is actually feeling. I can notice the changes in Jennifer's body language and in her expression. I can also notice that these changes make me feel less safe – maybe I've seen Jennifer start to push people in the past soon after she started acting like this. What's my safest choice right now, to stay next to her, or to get some space?.....Yes, I can leave! I can go to another game or another group of kids, or I can go do something on my own."

Don't Be There
Using target denial will prevent most forms of bullying. In workshops, we tell children, "A kid who is trying to bully you wants to cause trouble. Good target denial means not being there for that trouble either physically, with your body, or emotionally, with your feelings.

You don't want someone else's behavior to scare you into being a victim or push you into starting a fight. Walking away from someone bullying is safer than staying put and getting cornered. Walking away is also safer than escalating a situation by shoving someone out of your way or calling names."

The Have-a-Nice-Day! Self-Defense Tactic
We then show how using target denial looks, with two instructors pretending to be kids at school. Marylaine pretends to be a kid who wants to bully Pervaiz. She strides over to Pervaiz and says, "I'm going to get you." The first time, Pervaiz cowers against the wall and lets Marylaine trap him.

As Marylaine pushes him against the wall, Pervaiz shifts into instructor mode

> *When people are trying to pick a fight, acting sincerely nice in response can be very effective.*

and asks the students, "If Marylaine wants trouble and I don't, which one of us is getting what she wants?"

"Marylaine is," the students say.

The second time, as Marylaine swaggers over to Pervaiz in a threatening way, Pervaiz reacts by shoving her out of the way and yelling, "LEAVE ME ALONE!" Marylaine escalates by raising her fist as if she is about to fight. Pervaiz then goes back into instructor mode and asks, "If I don't want trouble and Marylaine does, and my reaction started a fight, who got what she wanted here, Marylaine or me?"

"She did," the students say.

The third time Marylaine starts to approach Pervaiz, he doesn't wait. He immediately leaves the wall moving away with awareness, calm, and confidence. He cheerfully waves and says, "Have a nice day!"

"Get back here, you wimp!" Marylaine shouts.

"No, thanks," Pervaiz says, as he continues to leave with awareness.

When people are trying to pick a fight, acting sincerely nice in response can be very effective. The key is to stay calm and centered rather than passive or aggressive. Using a mocking tone of voice or making a sarcastic gesture will probably make problems bigger. The best approach is to give a bully nothing to react to – neither fear nor anger.

Three generations of confident women!

What *Most Mothers* Prefer

This idea that leaving can be powerful instead of weak is especially important for teenagers, who sometimes feel that their honor is at stake if they don't have the last word. One of our Kidpower graduates was walking down the street with his friend. Some older boys drove by in a car shouting insults about their mothers. The Kidpower graduate immediately ran into a store to get help. Instead of going with him, the other boy started shouting threats to the boys in the car, who pulled over and beat him up so badly that he ended up in the hospital.

In this story, the boy who got beaten up was triggered by the insult about his mother. We ask our students, "What do you think the mother of the boy who was beaten up would have preferred – that her son defend her honor or get to safety?" If students say that they are not sure, we encourage them to ask their own mothers. I have yet to meet a mother who would rather have her honor defended than risk the safety of her child.

Walking Past Trouble

Instructor Eda explains to her students, "Imagine that I am a kid at school who is always insulting others and looking for trouble." Eda slouches in the middle of the room with her arms crossed, nodding her head and glaring. She coaches each student to walk across the floor, veering to get out of her way.

As the student goes by, Eda calls out insults like, "Scared, aren't you?" Or, "Hey stupid get over here!" Or, "I want to talk with you, wimp!" Or, "Look at the dumb freak!" Or, "*Bleep*, you *bleeping bleep*, you!"

If students need help, Eda interrupts the role-play to coach them to be successful. She says, "Keep walking. Walk tall. Use your imaginary Trash Can to throw away what this person is saying. Look back. Go to Safety."

When students get to the other side of the room, they each say out loud the compliment they are giving themselves to take the place of the insults.

The Fallacy of "Giving As Good As You Get"

Young people often think that they have to push or threaten back to defend their honor and to protect themselves. Many adults reinforce this belief. This is a dangerous belief, especially for young men in our culture. Men are at highest risk of getting stabbed or shot in their teens and early twenties. Many of these incidents start off with threats and pushes and then escalate into dangerous confrontations.

Remember that bullying situations are often chronic and usually involve people who students have to see again. The truth is that "giving as good as you get" by fighting back might stop a confrontation at the moment. The problem is that this response also increases the risk of escalated retaliation on another day. Using Target Denial will stop most situations as effectively if not more so than having an aggressive response, and with less risk of retaliation. This can also be true of an assertive response that sets a boundary but does not directly attack the honor of the other person.

Practicing Using Target Denial to Prevent Bullying

1   For children who are dealing with this kind of problem, find out what insults or threats the child wants to practice throwing away. Have the child stand in a corner of the room. If you do not have permission from the child's adults (depending on the situation, the child's parents, caregivers or teachers) to use the actual words, agree that the word "*Bleep!*" means whatever words this child might find most hard to walk away from.

2   Pretend to be a bully. Shout the agreed-upon insults or threats at the child while walking towards the child. You can glare and point your finger at the child without touching the child.

3   Coach the child to walk firmly away from you as soon as you start to approach, to throw the words away, to look back towards you with a friendly smile, to wave a hand, and to say something like, "Bye! Have a nice day! See you later!" – and keep on walking. Do the same practice standing in the middle of the room with the child veering to get around you while staying out of reach.

4   As the child is leaving, shake your fist and shout, "Come back here, you wimp!"

5   Coach the child to look back at you, to wave again, and to say cheerfully, "No thanks!" If necessary, remind the child to be sincere, not silly or sarcastic.

6   Ask the child how he or she was getting rid of the hurting words and what compliments he or she was using inside to replace the insulting language.

Chapter Six
Conflict Resolution and Interventions to Solve Problems

Conflict resolution techniques can help solve many relationship problems.

What Is Meant by "Conflict Resolution"
What Is a Mediator?
Negotiation Buddies
When Adults Don't Do Anything
Mixed Messages
Interventions to Prevent Conflict From Escalating
Teaching Young People How to Use Conflict Resolution Skills To Prevent Bullying

Conflict is a necessary and important part of most healthy relationships. People have different points of view and different needs. Learning how to work disagreements out in an effective fashion is a tremendous life skill. By promoting respect and looking for win-win solutions, using conflict resolution tools can create a climate where bullying is less likely to take place and more likely to be addressed quickly when it does.

However, bullying is not a part of a healthy relationship. Bullying takes place between people of unequal power, is usually repeated, and has the intent to be harmful. We would not ask adults who have been assaulted to sit down and have a discussion with their assailants. Forcing young people to engage in a conflict resolution process with those who has been bullying them can be emotionally devastating. Adult supervision and interventions are necessary when a child or teen is being bullied as well as to prevent escalation when a conflict cannot be resolved.

What Is Meant by "Conflict Resolution"
Children who understand and can use conflict resolution techniques will be able to solve many relationship problems. Conflict resolution programs for youth and adults have many basic concepts and skills in common. A good program should encourage participants to:

• Understand that conflict is a normal part of life and that knowing how to resolve conflict is a powerful life skill. Common personal conflicts are about our space, what we say to each other, our property, how we do activities together, and our time. Resolving conflicts can be an opportunity to learn about each other and to develop problem-solving skills.

• Understand the difference between passive, aggressive, and assertive ways of handling conflict.

40   **www.kidpower.org**

- Agree on ground rules for the conflict resolution process – no putdowns, no name-calling, making a commitment to solving the problem, and telling the truth.

- Communicate issues through specific, respectful "I" messages. For example, "I feel (name specific feeling), when you (name specific behavior). Would you please?" (State exactly what you want the other person to do or not do.)

- Listen respectfully, work to understand, and communicate your understanding back to the person. This requires using active listening, empathic listening, and apologies when appropriate as well as asking good questions. Respond with your own "I" message.

- Come up with lots of choices that help resolve the conflict in ways that follow the school, family, or youth group rules. Try to find solutions that give each person at least part of what he/she wants.

- Think of pros and cons of each choice and come to a mutual decision that both parties will agree to uphold.

- Thank each other for listening and reaching an agreement.

The most effective programs teach a system for using these ideas and skills to resolve conflicts at all levels. Role-plays are used so that people can rehearse how to use these skills to handle typical conflicts.

What Is a Mediator?

A mediator is a neutral, impartial third party whose role is to guide people through a conflict resolution process. The goal is to help opposing parties come up with their own solutions to resolving the conflict.

A mediator can be a teacher, a parent, another trusted adult, or a child.

A mediator's job typically involves the following process:

- Laying the groundwork by meeting with the opposing parties separately to allow them to ventilate, to set objectives, and to prepare them for the mediation. A mediator needs to use active listening and to ask neutral, supportive questions such as: "What do you want to see happen?" "What is the worst that could happen?" "What is the best that could happen?"

- Facilitating positive communication during the mediation session by welcoming the participants, being clear about the ground rules, giving each person a chance to tell his or her story, using active listening and supportive questions to make sure that each person feels that her or his perspective is understood, brainstorming different options, discussing the pros and cons of each possibility, looking for win-win solutions where each side gets at least some benefit, coming to an agreement, making a plan for what to do in case the agreement doesn't work, putting the agreement into writing, and thanking the participants for their commitment to creating a more peaceful world.

- Following up with each party to see how things are going.

A wealth of resources and tools are available in this field for teaching mediation and conflict resolution skills both to adults and to children.

Negotiation Buddies

Some schools train children to be mediators. My niece started her training as a "Negotiation Buddy" in the second grade. At age seven, she explained how it works: "When a kid gets mad at another kid, they put their names on the blackboard. It gets very busy because you get a lot of appointments during recess. You take the kid who was mad and the other kid to a quiet place so nobody will bother you. You help the mad kid fill out a card the teacher gives us that have an 'I' message to say what the mad kid feels and wants. The mad kid gives the card to the other kid who says, 'Yes, I will do what you want.' The mad kid isn't mad anymore and says, 'Thank you for listening.'"

"What happens when that doesn't work?" I wondered.

With utter faith that adults would take care of things, my seven-year-old niece said confidently, "Then we get the teacher!"

When Adults Don't Do Anything

Sadly, within a few years, my niece was disillusioned about the effectiveness of conflict resolution training. Too often in her life, kids had not wanted to work things out and adults had not known what to do. Talking it out and making agreements only work if there are clear boundaries defining acceptable behavior and realistic consequences for breaking the agreements made. For children who are bullying to get attention, "talking it out" can become a reward rather than a deterrent.

I have run into many children who have the same feeling – that conflict resolution is a good idea but it doesn't really work. "Sure, some kids who bully talk it out, but when they don't do what they promised, nothing happens," children will explain to me. "Sometimes the teacher is standing right there, but just ignores it. Or lectures them and then walks away. This kind of kid waits until the teacher isn't looking and then does it again."

This perception is unfortunate, because conflict resolution skills can often make a great difference in solving problems between people. Children need to see these as tools that work in some situations but not in others. We say that conflict resolution and boundary-setting skills are two sides of the same coin.

Adults can help prevent kids from getting disillusioned by:

• Ensuring that they have realistic expectations by explaining that, useful as conflict resolution skills can be, nothing works all the time.

• Celebrating successes - even small ones - in a highly public way.

• Teaching them to persist in finding solutions and in getting adult help. If problems don't get solved right away, this is a time to try different choices rather than giving up.

• Intervening to stop bullying by leading kids to do something positive,

No matter how much time, money, and effort you put into your anti-bullying program, nothing is going to work if kids see adults ignoring bullying when it happens in front of them!"

setting boundaries, coaching kids to practice safer behavior, or, when necessary, being consistent about consequences.

• Staying aware of the fact that maintaining a physically and emotionally safe environment for kids is an adult responsibility. Effective conflict resolution programs create outstanding opportunities for young people to learn powerful, lifelong skills. They can also engage young people in an age-appropriate way in creating a positive, caring group climate. However, no matter how effective a conflict resolution program is, the adults are always responsible for safety. This means they need to be ready to step in and help if kids are getting frustrated or disillusioned or if the process is breaking down.

Mixed Messages

During her Kidpower workshops for teachers, Senior Instructor Erika Leonard uses this example: "Imagine that it is 3:30 on the Friday before a holiday weekend. I've been at school since 6 a.m., and I'm exhausted. As I'm heading to the parking lot to go home, I see a cluster of parents talking and, completely unnoticed directly next to them, one child taunting another. What kinds of thoughts and feelings might get in the way of my stopping this behavior?"

Teachers sigh and say that a teacher in that position is likely to think:

• "These parents are supposed to be watching their kids!"
• "It's not my job!"
• "I already have to do too much. I can't do any more."
• "I'm not sure what to do. What if I make it worse or offend the parents?"
• "I've been with children all day and I'm DONE!"

"These feelings are normal," Erika says. "But, if children are being hurtful to each other and they believe adults notice but are choosing to do nothing, what are they learning about the meaning of the "Respect' and "Safety" posters around the school? No matter how much time, money, and effort you put into your anti-bullying program, nothing is going to work if kids see adults ignoring bullying when it happens in front of them!"

Interventions to Prevent Conflict From Escalating

As with other dangerous behaviors, adults need to know how and when to intervene when young people are in conflict. Parents need to be clear that bullying is against their family rules. Teachers and school officials need to be clear that bullying is against the school rules.

Adults need to show that they mean what they say by stopping bullying behavior with the same commitment that they would show to stop someone from throwing all the dishes on the floor and breaking them. As adults, we need to walk our talk by not allowing people to bully us and by exercising the self-control necessary not to bully others.

When young people are extremely upset, they might not be able to "talk it out" at first. They might need time and adult help to calm down and get perspective before they can participate in a conflict resolution process. Rather than ignoring a problem until it explodes, stepping in to give adult help before young people lose control of their tempers supports children in being successful.

Stepping in might mean:

• Creating a temporary distraction by bringing positive energy to a negative situation. You can buy yourself a little time by saying something very cheerfully like, "Hi! What did you think of the game last night?" Or, "Hey, how've you been?" Once things are calmer, you can then find out what was going on.

• Setting a boundary. "I understand that you are upset. You have the right to your feelings, and we can work on the problem. Please express yourself in a way that is respectful to others."

• Redirecting young people by getting them to do something with you instead of continuing to bother each other.

• Separating the aggressor from the other child or children.

Interventions can be done in a compassionate way rather than a punitive one. For example, "Oh my! You sound upset. I really want to understand what's going on. Let's go over here where it's quiet so we can talk about what happened."

Amy Tiemann, who is a Kidpower instructor and also a mother, tells the following story about an in-the-moment intervention:

"Putting Kidpower skills into practice has taught me that a successful intervention can sometimes happen in just a couple of seconds. I was on the school playground at a weekend social event attended by a large group of families. I noticed that two nine-near old classmates, a girl and a boy, were running in my general direction. The girl was moving away from her classmate and clearly telling him to stop, that their game was not fun any more.

"As they passed by where I was standing, the boy raised his hand to reach out to grab the girl, and I very simply put my hand out to deflect his grab, and stated in a calm, firm voice, "She said 'Stop'" This stopped his grab, defused the situation, and the kids went their own ways. The boy's mother saw what had almost happened and came over to talk to her son.

I was grateful to have Kidpower skills because the background preparation was key in training me to react in this moment. Sometimes we might worry that an intervention might be complicated or difficult, but I have found that often, Kidpower skills can be used to redirect situations before they become big problems.

The multiplier effect of simple actions like these can be enormous. Building a common understanding about the importance of putting safety first and a set of skills for acting on this understanding can make the difference between Safe and Unsafe for all of us in our relationships, families, schools, organizations, work places, and communities.

Working together to minimize conflict.

Teaching Young People How to Use Conflict Resolution Skills

1 Learn conflict resolution, negotiation, and mediation skills for yourself. For example, School Mediation Associates (http://www.schoolmediation.com/) offers books, articles, and a free e-newsletter.

2 Research systems of conflict resolution training for all parties to learn. Be sure that any program you select includes role-playing to develop skills and backup plans in case the conflict resolution process isn't working.

3 Teach young people about the conflict resolution process:
- State concerns assertively and respectfully;
- Listen to the other person's perspective and be able to re-state it accurately and compassionately;
- Brainstorm different ways of solving the problem;
- Look at pros and cons of different choices;
- Find win-win solutions where everyone gets at least part of what was wanted;
- Put agreements into writing;
- Appreciate oneself and others for being committed to conflict resolution: and
- Ask for help when agreements don't work.

4 Intervene before young people lose their tempers. Help them calm down before trying to work on problem-solving and conflict resolution solutions.

5 See the chapter on *Practice as a Management Tool for Unsafe, Disrespectful Behavior* for ideas about how to address problems in a way that builds skills for everyone.

6 Set clear boundaries to stop bullying and other unsafe behaviors. Do not force a child who has been bullied to be part of a conflict resolution process.

Chapter Seven

Self-Protection Skills to Avoid Being Pushed, Tripped, Bumped, Hit, Kicked, or Shoved

Learning how to set clear boundaries.

Making the Safest Choice
Stepping Out of the Way
Regaining Your Balance
Are You Trapped or Free to Leave?
Ready Position
Setting Boundaries and Yelling for Help
The Cower Power Game
Practicing Self-Protection Techniques to Stay Safe From
Threatening or Physically Aggressive Behavior

Sometimes kids get into fights because they are so afraid that someone might hurt them that they hit or kick as soon as they feel threatened or bothered. Starting a fight can cause them to be the ones to get into trouble, even if they are being constantly harassed by someone bullying them. Other kids worry a lot about being intimidated and keep hoping that it won't happen again. These young people benefit greatly from practicing skills to avoid and stop this kind of trouble.

Making the Safest Choice
When adults are not able to help, young people need to find the safest way to protect themselves. As thirteen-year-old Richard explained to me about an incident that happened after he had taken one of our workshops, "I should have known better than to keep going. I saw a group of guys from my school in a narrow street near downtown. I knew they were mad at me because I had told on one of them for cheating, but I just didn't feel like going out of my way.

"When these guys started pushing and hitting me, I knew that if I fought back, I would have more trouble the next day. Instead, I protected myself by shielding my face and body. I practiced false surrender by apologizing even though I didn't do anything wrong. Next time, I will use my awareness and go the other way instead of challenging people who are upset with me by walking right through them."

Richard understood that, although this attack was not his fault, using his awareness could have protected him from these boys who were looking for trouble.

Even under the stressful circumstances of being hit and shoved, Richard felt good that, after his initial mistake of getting too close, he was able to stay centered in order to decide on the safest way to prevent future conflict. He discussed what happened with his parents. They decided that taking further action about these boys in this particular neighborhood was not in his best interest. Fortunately, Richard was able to avoid these boys and soon afterwards changed schools.

This was not a perfect solution from my perspective. I would far rather have had Richard and his parents feel able to tell the police and his school what happened. Realistically, however, their solution might well have been the safest way for Richard to handle the problem.

Stepping Out of the Way

When students are hurrying through the hall or busy playing in a crowded school, they have plenty of opportunities to bother each other. After she started going to a new school, eleven-year-old Angela was coming home with bruises caused by a few girls who kept bumping into her "accidentally" and knocking her down.

Angela's father said, "I asked Angela if she knew who these girls were. She did but she did not want me to do anything about it. So, I asked her to show me what the girls looked like before they started to bump into her. When she did, I was able to step out of the way easily. Next, we practiced with my taking on the role of the girls. We made it a game for me to start towards Angela and for her to move calmly out of the way. The problem at school stopped. Once she gave herself permission to pay attention and to act on what she was noticing, Angela had no problem avoiding being bumped without needing to confront anybody."

Regaining Your Balance

In places where shoving is an issue, we teach students how to keep their feet under them and leave rather than shoving back or getting into a fight. Instructors Ron and Janice show their class how leaving in an assertive way rather than becoming aggressive or passive can work in this situation.

Janice says, "Imagine that we are two people about your age who know each other. Ron is in a bad mood." She and Ron stand close together facing each other. Suddenly, Ron pushes Janice and she staggers backwards, pretending to lose her balance.

Janice moves back to face Ron and he pushes her again. This time, Janice reacts aggressively by making her shoulder rigid, so it seems as if she is shoving back. Janice and Ron then glower and point at each other, snapping, "Hey, cut it out!"

"Next, we're going to look at all the choices I have instead of losing my balance or shoving back," Janice tells her class.

This time when Ron pushes her, Janice lets the force of the shove turn her body away without being rigid or pushing back. She then walks away with awareness.

When Ron pushes her again, Janice steps to one side to get out of the way and leaves with awareness.

One last time, Janice gets shoved. She goes backwards with the force of the shove in a balanced way by moving her feet so that they stay under her. Once she is out of the way, Janice again leaves with awareness.

When they give their students the chance to practice, Ron and Janice push gently so that the students will be successful.

Are You Trapped or Free to Leave?
Too often, people get stuck in unsafe situations because they don't realize that they are able to leave. Janice shows students the difference between being trapped and being free to leave.

The Kidpower Ready Position.

She creates an imaginary doorway, using two chairs. Janice then says, "Imagine that this is the doorway to a bathroom. Outside the bathroom is Safety, in the school or the house where other people are. Inside, it is less safe. The doorway is the only way to leave."

Ron stands in the doorway of the "bathroom" waving his fist and making threatening noises. Janice stands outside and shows that she is free to leave. In fact, she has no reason to stay near this guy when he is acting so obnoxiously. She walks away calmly, looking back.

Next, Janice moves inside the bathroom so that Ron is blocking the doorway. Just leaving is not a choice for Janice at this point, because Ron is trapping her. Janice shows how she might still decide to duck under his arm or push past him and leave. However, since Ron is showing a clearly aggressive intent, getting closer to him might make things more dangerous for her.

Ron and Janice give each student the opportunity to practice, so they can experience the difference between being trapped and being free to leave.

Ready Position
Without practice, most people when confronted by someone who is threatening them often act either weak or aggressive, which is likely to make the problem worse. We are safest if we get ready to deal with the problem. The purpose of the Ready Position we teach in Kidpower is to communicate to the other person that we are not a victim, nor a threat, nor a challenge - we are simply ready.

To get into Ready Position, stand with your feet a little a part as if you've just stopped walking, so that you are in balance. Put your two hands in front of you, palms facing out, hands open, elbows bent, as if you were touching a wall several inches away from your body. This is your Ready Position. You are ready to leave, ready to set a boundary, and ready to yell for help. If you need to do this to protect yourself, you are also ready to fight to stop someone from harming you.

Setting Boundaries and Yelling for Help
After teaching her students the Ready Position, Janice then goes back to

the demonstration of being trapped inside the bathroom. She explains, "Since awareness and target denial have not worked, I am going to let this person know that I am not an easy victim and let the world know that I have a problem."

As Ron pretends to mock and threaten her from the doorway, Janice steps back out of his reach. She gets into Ready Position and shouts, "STOP! GET OUT OF MY WAY! I NEED HELP! RON IS TRAPPING ME IN THE BATHROOM!" Not wanting to get into trouble, Ron leaves, muttering threats.

Janice and Ron have all the students get into Ready Position and practice setting strong boundaries such as, "*Stop! Don't push me! Go away! Don't follow me!* I NEED HELP!"

In the context of a bullying problem, students review the importance of using a clear, strong, assertive tone of voice; choosing words carefully; and keeping their bodies aware, calm, and confident. They all make the same statements, leaning back and sounding whiny or weak. They repeat the exercise, leaning forward and getting into the other person's face, acting as if they want to fight. Finally, they stand or sit upright, repeating the statements with a firm face, a calm definite tone, and a loud voice.

In a school situation, where the bothering is constant, setting boundaries is often effective even if you are not trapped physically. Shirley D. Kassebaum, a counselor at Watson Junior High School, wrote a letter that illustrates this fact. "One of the boys who participated in your workshop used to see me on the average of two or three times a week to complain about someone picking on him. Not long ago, I observed him in the lunch line. The kid in front of him pushed him. He put up his hands up into Ready Position and said, in a loud voice, 'Stop! I don't like to be pushed!'"

The Cower Power Game
In order to build belief in the power of sounding and looking like you mean it, we sometimes demonstrate and then play what we call the "Cower Power Game" in our workshops. We have students stand in two lines facing a partner. Instructor Timothy says, "The first time, those of you in the line on this side are the Bullies and your partners are the Kids."

He directs the Bullies to shake their fingers at their partners and, without touching them, to move aggressively towards them shouting, 'BLAH! BLAH! BLAH!"

Timothy directs the Kids to cower away, with their heads down and their backs turned to the Bullies, whimpering, "Please don't hurt me! Please don't hurt me!"

Timothy then calls the group back into their two lines. This time, when the Bullies advance, the Kids shake their fingers and yell, "BLAH! BLAH! BLAH!" back. Since no one is allowed to touch each other, each pair ends up stuck in shaking, glaring, and yelling.

Timothy asks, "Does this look familiar?" and everyone laughs.

Once again, Timothy has the groups re-form their lines. This time, he tells the Kids to step back into Ready Position, to make a Stop Sign by moving one hand out and back towards the face of their Bully partner without touching anyone. He makes sure that the lines are far enough apart from each other so that when a Stop Sign goes forward, the face of the Bully is at least a few feet away. He coaches the Kids to shout "STOP!" when they make the Stop Sign.

The Kidpower Stop Sign.

The Bullies move a step or two towards their partners aggressively, shouting. Following Timothy's directions, the Kids get into Ready Position, make their Stop Signs, and yell, "STOP!" Most of the Bullies will act startled, even though they knew what was going to happen.

After the Bullies and the Kids have switched roles so that everyone gets to try both parts of the exercise, Timothy calls the group together for discussion. "When you were the Kid and acted like a victim, how did you feel inside?" Regardless of their culture or age, most students say things like, "Weak." "Scared." "Helpless." "Stupid."

"And," Timothy continues, "When you were the Bully and your partner cowered away, how did you feel?"

"Strong," his students reply, "like I could keep going."

"What about when you and your partner were both shouting and shaking your fingers at each other? " Timothy asks, "How did that feel?"

"Like the other person started it," his students from both groups typically say, "and as if I couldn't figure out how we ended up there."

"How did it feel," Timothy continues, "to be the Kid and to get into Ready Position and to shout 'STOP'?"

"Strong," his students say. "Like I was in charge." And, "Like I had the space to leave."

Finally, Timothy asks, "And when you were the Bully and your partner used the Stop Sign and shouted at you to stop. How did you feel?"
With a look of realization, most of his students say, "I felt surprised." "I felt like I was the one who was stupid." Or, "I felt stopped, even though I knew it was going to happen."

50   **www.kidpower.org**

Practicing Self-Protection Techniques to Stay Safe From Threatening or Physically Aggressive Behavior

When a young person has a problem, here's how to how to practice dealing with it:

1   Find out the specifics of exactly what is being said or done. Have the child or teen show you what the problem behavior of the other person looks like and sounds like.

2   Make a plan for using awareness, staying centered, leaving, getting help, and using assertive boundary setting to solve the specific problem. See the *Assertive Advocacy* section on pages 122-126 for more about the differences between being passive, aggressive, and assertive..

3   If pushing or tripping is the problem, let young people practice keeping their balance by stepping out of the way, moving their feet to get them back under their bodies, or letting the force of the push move them away. In each case, add leaving with awareness so that they get used to moving away from someone who is creating problems. When you practice, start with a very gentle shove so that young people can be successful.

4   Play the "Cower Power Game" described above in order to build belief. To ensure safety, remember that no one touches each other in this game. Keep enough space between the lines to allow the Stop Sign to go forward and back while still leaving a few feet of space between the extended hand and the other person's face.

Chapter Eight
Getting Adults to Help

Why Kids Don't Ask for Help
Tools for Getting Help
How **You Ask for Help Matters**
When to Wait and When to Interrupt
Be a Helpful Adult to Talk To
Adults Are the Ones In Charge
Teaching Young People How to Get the Attention of Busy Adults

Especially as they get older, young people often become discouraged and frustrated about the ability of their adults to help them solve problems with other kids. We tell our students that nothing works all the time. We explain that, even if they are distracted and busy, most adults care about their kids a lot and want them to be safe and happy.

We have found that this is true of most families and schools. Their children are the most important part of their lives, but parents, other adult family members, and school staff get so overwhelmed with the sheer magnitude of conflicting demands that they don't notice a problem or they have unrealistic expectations of what a child can do without adult help.

This is why we teach young people to persist in asking for help as effectively as possible. This is also why adults need to show kids that they are going to be helpful people to come to with problems and to make sure that young people are in environments where bullying is truly against the rules and where the rules are enforced.

Why Kids Don't Ask for Help
In order to increase our own understanding, we asked children who had struggled with safety problems alone what had stopped them from getting help. Here are some typical answers:

• *I thought my teacher knew*. A five-year-old girl who was having her dress pulled up by boys during recess said, "It happened right in front of the teacher. I thought she knew."

• *I'm not supposed to interrupt*. A ten-year-old boy, who got hurt because his safety bar wasn't working at an amusement park, told his mother later, "The ticket lady was very busy, and I know I'm not supposed to interrupt."

• *My teacher told me to fix it myself*. A seven-year-old boy, who eventually got too upset to go to school because kids were making fun of him during recess, explained, "I did tell the teacher, but he told me that I should work things out myself and not be so whiny."

• *Everybody said it was just a joke*. An eight-year-old girl, who was getting

As they get older, young people often become discouraged and frustrated about the ability of their adults to help them solve problems with other kids.

hurt by constant unkind jokes from an older cousin at a family gathering, sighed, "I tried to explain how I felt, but no one paid any attention. They said that my cousin was just kidding."

- *I wanted to be able to keep seeing my friend.* A nine-year-old girl, who was scared of the aggressive brother of her best friend, said, "My parents were always so busy worrying about their own problems that I didn't want to bother them. Also, I was afraid they wouldn't let me go to my friend's house anymore."

- *I didn't know the words to say.* A group of ten-year-olds who were scared because the driver of their car on a field trip with their youth group was drunk and driving poorly, explained after they crashed that, "We were too embarrassed to tell anybody. Also, we didn't know what to say or who to say it to."

- *My Dad told me not to complain.* An eleven-year-old boy, who started to hate soccer because his coach kept pushing him to try harder even though he kept getting injured, said, "I tried to tell my Dad, but every time I said anything, he gave me a big lecture about not wimping out just because of a little pain."

- *I felt embarrassed.* "I'm in high school now. When kids on the team were pushing me around, I felt like I should be able to handle this myself."

- *My Mom got terribly upset.* An eleven-year-old girl, whose classmates were making inappropriate sexual comments to her, eventually explained, "My mom got so upset the first time I told her about a problem at school that she kept worrying all the time and complaining to everybody else about it in a way that embarrassed me. I decided it was easier to try to solve my own problems."

- *I didn't want to get into trouble.* A twelve-year-old boy, who had been followed and threatened by a group of older kids, said, "I promised my friends that I wouldn't say anything because we'd gone downtown instead of staying at the park like we were supposed to. I wanted to be loyal to my friends, and I was afraid that I would get into trouble myself."

- *I was afraid.* A group of sixth graders, who saw a student threatening another student with a knife after school, explained after one got hurt and the other got arrested, "We were afraid that someone would get back at us if we said anything."

From a young person's perspective, these reasons make sense. If we want children to believe differently, we need to tell them explicitly that we want them to come to us for help, give them tools for getting help, and be helpful adults for them to come to.

Tools for Getting Help
The tools children need for getting help include knowing how to:

1. *Find an adult who will listen and help.* Knowing how to find adults who will help you in different places is part of your safety plan.

2. *Get the attention of busy adults.* Even if adults are looking right at you, they might not understand that you are having a problem. If you are being bullied and an adult doesn't stop it, you have to speak up for yourself. When you have a safety problem, your job is to interrupt adults to get help, even though they are busy.

3. *Use a regular voice so that you sound respectful and firm rather than whiny or rude.* Remember to act calm, aware, and confident. You can say, "Excuse me. I need help. I have a safety problem." Explain what the problem is.

4. *If the adult doesn't listen at first, be persistent – this means not giving up – and ask again.* Other people cannot read your mind, so you will need to tell the whole story about what happened. Children, especially young children, often think that adults can read their minds. Since the adults around them always seem to know when they are tired, hungry, or upset, this makes sense. Children need to understand that, even if their adults understand them really well, their adults cannot read their minds and know what all of their problems or concerns are. This is why children need to practice telling adults the whole story (what, where, and when the problem happened; why they are worried, upset, or scared, etc.).

5. *If one adult will not help you even though you have really tried, then find another adult.* Keep asking for help until somebody understands and gives you the help you need.

How You Ask for Help Matters

Kidpower teacher Stefany tells her students, "Remember that you can ask for help if you are having trouble with other people at school. But how you talk with an adult can make a difference in how much attention the adult gives you."

Stefany coaches her students to repeat after her, modeling the tone of voice she wants them to use, "Everybody say in a whiny voice, 'Teeeeacherrrrr! They're bothering meeeeee.'"

She asks her students, "Do you think teachers like to listen to you when you talk like that? Do you like listening to yourselves?"

"No," everyone agrees.

Stefany then shows students how to make a report, asking ten-year-old Raul, who has done this before, to help her demonstrate. Stefany sets the stage by saying, "Suppose that I am a teacher and a couple of kids have kept following Raul around and bothering him on the school yard."

Stefany pretends to be talking to another teacher. Because he needs help, Raul interrupts by saying very politely, "Excuse me. I have a safety problem."

Playing the role of the teacher, Stefany firsts acts as if she doesn't hear and continues to be busy.

Raul persists by saying in a louder voice, sounding firm and respectful, rather

No matter what age they are, children and teens need good skills on how to effectively ask for help.

than whiny, "Excuse me! I need help!"

"What *now*?" Stefany demands impatiently.
Raul stays calm and says seriously, "I have a safety problem and I need your help. I want to make a report."
Stefany looks surprised. "A report? About what?" she asks.

Raul gives a full report to describe his problem by explaining, "A couple of kids from another class keep pointing, bumping into me, and calling me names. I didn't answer and tried to leave, but they followed me. I moved away but they followed me. I asked them to stop, but they didn't. Please help me."

Stefany becomes sympathetic and says, "You tried really hard to solve this problem yourself. I am glad you told me, and I am sorry that I was impatient. With so many people out sick, this has been a hard day. You have the right to feel safe at school, so let's make a plan to stop this from happening."

Stefany then has students practice individually or as a group, picking different problems and adult roles. She reminds them that their job is to stay calm and clear when they give their report, tell the whole story, use a firm, polite tone of voice, and have confident body language. She coaches them to not give up even when the adult acts annoyed, impatient, or rude.

Sometimes, Stefany interrupts the student by saying, "That's not so bad. Just ignore it." Or, "What's the big deal? Just stay away from them." She coaches students to tell the whole story, including what they had tried, and to persist in explaining the problem. For example, "I have the right to be safe at school. This is bullying, and I've done what I know how to do. Now, I need your help."

Finally, as the adult, Stefany listens and says, "Thank you for telling me. We will figure out how to help you feel safe at school." She reminds students that if the adult they are supposed to go to for help still doesn't listen, their job is to find another adult.

When to Wait and When to Interrupt

Sometimes in solving one problem, you create another. Early in our program development for Kidpower, we learned that children need clear boundaries about using the "being persistent in getting help" skill. When we became very successful in teaching children how to get the attention of busy adults, their parents and teachers started to complain that these children were interrupting them very effectively all the time. They pointed out that they had been helping children learn how to wait instead of demanding constant, immediate attention, and now we were teaching them how to interrupt!

We now teach children that they often have to *wait* when they *want* something, but that their safety rule is to *interrupt* and *keep asking* if they *need help* with a safety problem.

We describe what this means using situations relevant to their lives, such as, "In public, you *wait* at the end of the line when you *want* to buy something. But, you go to the front of the line and *interrupt* and *keep asking* if you *need help* because you are lost or don't feel safe."

An example for a younger child might be, "Suppose your mom is on the phone. If you want to play a game, do you *wait* or *interrupt*? That's right, you wait. But what if the pot is boiling over on the stove? That's a safety problem, and you interrupt."

For an older child, the example could be, "Suppose that your teacher is busy talking to another teacher. If you want to ask questions about your homework, do you *wait* or *interrupt*? That's right, you wait. But suppose your friend is throwing up in the bathroom? Yes, that's a safety problem, and you interrupt."

Children will be safer if the adults in their lives tell them clearly, "You can interrupt me or other adults with a safety problem, no matter how busy we are. Even if I tell you to leave me alone so I can get something done, I want you to interrupt me and keep asking if you need help. If a safety problem is really bothering you, you can even wake me up in the middle of the night!" Many families decide that the words, "This is about my safety!" will be a signal that warns adults to stop and listen right away.

Children need to have adults who will listen to their problems.

Be a Helpful Adult to Talk To

If we want young people to seek adult help, they need to feel safe coming to us with problems. When a young person asks for help, you might feel impatient because the problem seems trivial from your adult perspective. You might feel very upset because any risk or threat to the people you love can cause you to explode with feelings. No matter how you feel, remember that this situation can give this young person an opportunity to develop an understanding about the value of asking you for help.

Being a helpful adult to talk to means:

1. *Say, before anything else: "Thanks for telling me!"* No matter how busy you are, no matter what the child might have done wrong, you want to show appreciation to this child for having had the courage to tell you.

2. *Listen and ask open-ended supportive questions to make sure that you understand the whole story.* Nod. Make eye contact. Say, "Hmmm. Please tell me more." Ask, "What else happened?" Glaring and demanding to know, "*Why* did you do *that*?" is not asking a supportive question. Avoid asking leading questions, because children might say what they think you want them to say rather than explaining their true concerns.

3. *Stay calm.* Young people often want to protect their adults from getting upset. They are likely to feel alarmed if you sound hysterical or start making threats. They might even change their story to calm you down or be sorry that they said anything. Take a deep breath if you need to gather yourself. Instead of getting caught up in your feelings of the moment, think through the best ways to handle the situation with the big picture of what you want to accomplish in mind and what behavior you want to model.

4. *Don't lecture or scold, no matter what this young person might have done to cause the problem.* Later, after you have heard the whole story, you might decide that some consequences for misbehavior are necessary. If so,

be sure to also offer her or him some benefit for having had the courage to come and tell you.

5. *As much as possible, involve this young person in figuring out what to do and how to do it.* Remember that how you handle this situation will have a lot to do with whether or not you will be seen as a safe person to come to in the future. In addition, your job is to make sure that young people are in safe environments with safe people. This means that feelings of embarrassment must not stop you from taking action to make the situation better. Offer choices about *how* problems are solved, *not* about *whether* they are solved.

6. *When YOU need it, also get help.* The knowledge, skill, and experience of others can provide perspective and alternatives that might not occur to you. Also, you might need to find someone with the authority to take action in solving the problem.

Adults Are the Ones In Charge

Children who are being bullied need to be able to tell teachers and other adults in charge what is happening in the moment clearly, calmly, and persistently even if these adults are being rude and even if asking for help has not worked before. Using polite, firm words; showing assertive body language; keeping calm, firm tone of voice even under pressure; and persisting when asking for help are powerful skills that will help them throughout their lives.

Even more, children need the adults in schools to take responsibility for creating a safe environment for the children in their care. As caring adults, we must advocate for our children. Adults also need to use assertiveness skills by speaking up when something is wrong and skills to persist in seeking solutions even though others might minimize, ignore, or get upset with their concerns.

As caring adults, we must advocate for our children.

Teaching Young People How to Get the Attention of Busy Adults

1 Ask older children for whom this might be an issue to tell you about times when they asked adults for help and what worked or didn't. If they don't have an example at first, you might start with stories about what happened to you when you were a kid or about someone else. Maybe the adult got mad at them. Maybe the adult ignored them or looked away, or perhaps the adult overreacted and made things worse. Maybe telling the adult ended up giving them more problems with other kids, or maybe the adult was having a bad day.

2 Listen sympathetically to what kids tell you, even if you think their perceptions are wrong or unfair. Reflect back to them what they have said in a way that honors their perspective, so that they feel heard. Sometimes young people have lost trust in adult help. To gain the confidence to try again, they need to be able to tell their stories and to have their feelings acknowledged.

3 Show children how to use their assertiveness skills to be persistent, powerful, and respectful in making a report.

4 Give children the chance to take on the role of the harassed, impatient adult while you pretend to be a young person making a report. Then switch roles.

5 Remind children that, if the adult *still* does not listen, this is not their fault. Their job is to keep asking until someone does something to fix the problem. Tell the children in your life that you always want to know if they have a problem with anyone, anywhere, anytime, because you care, and you will do your best to help them.

6 Sometimes, the best way to help your child is to seek professional help. When children are having big problems, they often need a neutral adult to talk with because they are worried about upsetting one or both of their parents.

7 Create a Role-Play to Practice Being Persistent in Getting Help
 • Make up a safety problem that might be relevant to the young person you are teaching. For example, you might tell an elementary-aged child, "Imagine that some kids locked you in the bathroom at school, and you were scared and want to tell me about it."

 • Ask children if they have ever noticed that sometimes you and other adults are "Busy, busy, busy!" Ask the child you are practicing with what person he would go to if he had a safety problem. Very likely, he will say, "My mom." Ask him what his mom might be busy doing. Offer choices that you think would be

(Continued on next page.)

appropriate such as using the computer, washing the dishes, or reading.

- Start the practice by pretending to be his mom (or whatever adult he chooses) who is busy doing something. If you are practicing with your own child, think of something that you are often busy doing. Think of an activity that might be hard to interrupt. Pretend to be busy doing this activity.

- Coach the child to interrupt politely by saying, "Excuse me, Mom. I have a safety problem. Some kids locked me in the bathroom at school today, and I felt scared."

- Keep looking at what you are pretending to do and say obliviously, "Go ahead, honey! I'm listening. I'm glad you had a nice time at school."

- With pauses between the leading questions, ask, "Am I listening? No! Have you ever noticed that adults say, 'ummm hmmmm. That's nice. I'm listening,' when they are *not paying attention*? What do you need to know that your mom is listening?" Point to your eyes if he is not sure and say, "That's right. You need her to be looking at you."

- If you are doing this with your own child, do so in the first person by asking, "What do you need to see from me to know that I am listening?"

- Coach the child to touch your arm, look you in the eyes, and say, "Mom! Please look at me. I need help!"

- Pretend to get angry by glaring and snapping, *"Can't I have a minute's peace? I told you not to bother me when I'm busy!"*

- Ask leading questions that children can answer "Yes" to, such as, "Do adults sometimes get grumpy when you bother them while they are busy? Is it important to keep asking for help anyway?" Coach the child who is practicing to say again, "But this is about my safety. Some kids locked me in the bathroom at school."

- Get very interested and calm and say, "Oh, *why* didn't you tell me right away?" (Children enjoy being able to reply, "I did!") Let the child tell you the whole story, and then say, "Thank you for telling me. You did the right thing to interrupt me, and I'm sorry that I was grouchy with you. You deserve to be safe, and we'll figure out what to do."

Chapter Nine

Bully Self-Defense Techniques

Bully Tactics and Emergency-Only Tactics
Ask Your Adults
Pulling or Twisting Away to Escape
Bully Self-Defense Targets and Techniques
Success Stories
Preparing Young People to Use Bully Self-Defense Tactics

Most bullying can be stopped by setting boundaries, leaving and getting help. When this doesn't work, children need to know when they have the right to hurt someone to stop that person from hurting them. The rules about where to draw the line are very different in different families, which is why we encourage young people to discuss specific problems with their adults.

Bully Tactics and Emergency-Only Tactics

Kidpower teaches that fighting should be a last resort – when you are about to get hurt and you cannot leave or get help.

Often, bullying situations are not so clear-cut. In an attack or abduction, you are experiencing a very dangerous emergency in which you might be severely injured or even killed. In such circumstances, techniques such as eye-strikes that are likely to cause injury can be justified.

A bullying attack is often not an immediate emergency. Usually, leaving and getting to safety are possible choices. Although this is true, young people often ask the following "What if?" questions:

• "What if the kid follows you?"
• "What if the kid keeps on shoving you?"
• "What if the kid does it only when the teacher is not looking?"
• "What if you cannot get away without getting hurt first?"
• "What if kids push you down and grab your lunch money?"

At Kidpower, we tell children that getting away and getting adult help are the safest options whenever possible. If young people have permission from their adults to use physical self-defense skills and they cannot leave or get help, we acknowledge that the only way to protect themselves from getting hurt might be to fight back. For this reason, we have children practice "bully self-defense" techniques that are less likely to cause injury than the "emergency-only self-defense" techniques that we also teach.

Ask Your Adults

Unlike adults who can change their jobs, most young people do not have the

Fighting should be a last resort – when you are about to get hurt and you cannot leave or get help.

60   **www.kidpower.org**

Self-defense as a last resort.

choice to leave their schools. Every day at school or on the way to or from school, young people get knocked down, punched, kicked or have their hair pulled, their bottoms slapped, their heads smacked, their shoulders tapped hard, their clothes pulled off, and their breasts grabbed in a way that hurts and humiliates them.

Schools vary greatly in their ability to handle this kind of problem. Sometimes schools have a "no fighting" policy that leads to both children getting into trouble if someone fights back, no matter what the circumstances Families have very different boundaries about fighting back when you might get hurt, but not injured. This is why we tell children, "Ask your adults when it is okay to hurt someone to stop that person from hurting, shoving, or grabbing you."

One mother put her thirteen-year-old daughter Jasmine into a workshop because a boy at school was constantly grabbing Jasmine's breast. After the workshop, Jasmine's mother wrote a letter to the school principal that said, "You have failed to protect my daughter, so I have taken her to a program to teach her to protect herself. If she uses her skills to stop someone from harming her and you try to give her consequences, I will back her up, all the way to the school board if I have to."

Later Jasmine's mother told us that this boy had grabbed her daughter's breast and Jasmine had knocked the wind out of him with a heel palm strike to the mid-section, walked away immediately, and given her teacher a report about what had happened. The school did not punish Jasmine and, after that, the boy left her completely alone.

Pulling or Twisting Away to Escape

Young people can often escape physically from attacks without hurting the other person by:
- Pulling or twisting away from a grab;
- Dodging or blocking a punch; and
- Lifting their arms abruptly over their heads to raise their shoulders and turning their bodies to get out of a choke hold.

Since no one gets hurt, using these techniques has the advantage of reducing the likelihood of getting into trouble and of making the other person less likely to want to get even.

Bully Self-Defense Targets and Techniques

The following techniques are designed to give a short amount of pain with a lower risk of injuring someone, making enough space and time to get away. Literally hundreds of other physical techniques could also work, but these are very easy to learn.

The first two techniques start from Ready Position, with your body upright, both arms in front of you and close to your body, elbows bent, palms open and facing the attacker, and legs a step apart with your strong foot back.

- **Bully Soccer Kick to the Shin**. Rather than kicking forward with your toes, your "weapon" is the inner side of your foot, like in soccer. The target is the shin of the other person. If you have ever bumped your shin on the edge of a coffee table, you will know that this hurts. Kick forward to the shin with a loud "NO!"

- **Bully Heel Palm to the Solar Plexus**. Your target is towards the solar plexus or whatever you can hit on the middle of someone's body. If you have ever had the wind knocked out of you, you will know that this can be very effective. Your weapon is the heel or hard spot at the bottom of your palm. We do not recommend using your fists because there is a greater risk of injuring yourself. Keep your arm a little bent to avoid hyper-extending your arm. From Ready Position, hit forward with a loud "NO!" You can add power by taking a small step for-ward with your front foot and then sliding your back foot forward as you do the technique.

- **Low Elbow to the Solar Plexus**. This is useful if you are being grabbed from behind. Reach forward with your arm, turn your body to make room, and then jab backwards into the attacker's mid-section, hitting her or him with your elbow.

- **Bully Pinch**. Use your fingers to grab a small amount of flesh from the other person's upper arm or inner thigh. Pinch hard and twist. This can be an effective way to make someone who is trapping you in a headlock and rubbing your head to let go. You can pinch and twist any soft fleshy area. (*Carefully*, you can try this out on your own body if you want to test whether it works.)

After the children have learned these techniques in our workshops, we give them the chance to practice.

Our instructor pretends to be the Bully by moving close and saying threatening things like, "Do what I say or you'll be sorry!" Or, "Hey punk, I'm going to get you!" Or shaking a fist and muttering, "You're getting some of *this*!"

Each child practices, imagining a situation where leaving does not make sense, such as being trapped in a corner or room. The child first warns the "Bully" by standing in Ready Position, making a Stop Sign, and yelling, "LEAVE ME ALONE! I MEAN IT!" Next, the child delivers the Bully Kick to the shin or the Bully Heel Palm to the Solar Plexus with a loud "NO!" Finally, the child leaves quickly, imagining going to a safe adult and making a report.

If we let children practice using the pinch to get out of a headlock, we tell them, "Please just pinch our pants, not us!"

Success Stories
We have had many success stories about children using each of these techniques to put a stop to bullying.

As one father told us, "Every day at the swimming pool, my thirteen-year-old daughter was getting dunked under water by an older boy, supposedly in play. When he wouldn't listen to her, she pinched him under the arm. He never dunked her again."

Another father said, "My six-year-old daughter has curly red hair. Other kids can't resist sticking their fingers in it and pulling. She used to cry but, after

62   **www.kidpower.org**

> *Learning how to manage their triggers and control their power can help young people have an appropriate response to violence instead of overreacting.*

learning to protect herself, she stopped one very persistent little boy with a bully heel palm. After that, all the kids kept their hands to themselves."

One girl, aged nine, who lives in the inner city, said, "A bully on the playground grabbed my hair and pulled me backwards. I stopped him by elbowing him once in the stomach. The yard duty teacher complimented me on how I took care of myself without being a bully, too. She said she wished she knew how to do that."

Learning how to manage their triggers and control their power can help young people have an appropriate response to violence instead of overreacting. One mother put her thirteen-year-old son, Todd, into a Kidpower workshop because he kept getting into fights at school. "The principal says that Todd won't be able to go to the graduation if he gets into one more fight," she explained to me. "Todd says that he goes crazy because a group of other boys keeps bullying him and he gets scared. So, I am counting on Kidpower to help my son be in his middle school graduation."

I told her that we would try our best, but I couldn't make any promises. A few weeks after the workshop, Todd's mother called to say, "Thank you for helping my son graduate with his class. One of those boys grabbed Todd from behind and started hitting him. He did one low elbow to the midsection of the bully to make the boy let him go and then went to the teacher and made a report. After that, the boys have left him completely alone."

My own daughter, Chantal, at age twelve, once took my breath away by saying casually at dinner one evening, "By the way, Mom, I used my Kidpower today."

She and her friends were at the park that afternoon when a group of older boys from their school came by and started to bother them. These boys took their ball. The little brother of one of Chantal's friends said, "Give me back my ball!" Instead, a bigger boy started to twist the wrist of this little boy to make him kneel on the ground.

Seeing anyone's little brother hurt in front of her was unacceptable to Chantal. She got into Ready Position and yelled, "LEAVE HIM ALONE!" When the older boy came towards her, Chantal yelled, "LEAVE ME ALONE!" He kept coming, and she kicked him in the shin.

Chantal told me that she had thought, "If two of them come at me, that's an emergency and I am going to kick somebody in the groin."

Instead, the boy she kicked hopped away, yelling "Ow!" The other boys said, "What a powerhouse!" They tossed back the ball and went to the other side of the park.

At that time, Chantal was small and shy, and her friends were astounded. "We own the park!" they said. But Chantal thought about five boys regrouping and made her friends leave the park. She told me later that for the rest of the school year, the boy she had kicked made a big circle around her whenever they passed each other in the halls.

In each of the above situations, one strong move was enough to stop a serious bullying problem.

Much more often, though, adults tell us that the physical confidence gained from knowing self-defense has been enough for their children to deal with bullies without actually having to fight. One mother told us, "A couple of years ago, my son was injured so badly by bullies that he had to go to the hospital. After that, his victim behavior made him a continual target. Since taking a Kidpower class, he has used what he learned to stop eleven incidents with bullies without ever once having to resort to violence."

Preparing Young People to Make Appropriate Decisions and to Know How to Use Bully Self-Defense Tactics

1   Review with children all the different ways in which they can get out of a bullying situation without fighting.

2   Be sure that children know the difference between when they should use the Emergency-Only Self-Defense Tactics with target such as the groin, head, or eyes - and when they should use the Bully Self-Defense Tactics. Explain why some targets are less likely to cause injury than others.

3   Be specific with children about when you believe that they have the right to hurt someone who is trying to bully them physically.

4   Acknowledge possible consequences at school. Timothy Dunphy told his daughter that, if she had to hit someone to protect herself from bullying and then got into trouble for it, he would stay home with her and talk to the school officials.

5   Give children the opportunity to learn and practice the techniques described above. Consider having them take a class. See section on *How to Choose a Good Self-Defense Program* on pages 128-130.

Relational bullying is extremely hurtful.

Coping With Shunning, Exclusion, and Gossip

My Own Story
Relational Bullying
Adjusting Emotional Distance
The "I'd Like to Join the Game" Practice
The Meet-New-People Personal Safety Tactic
The Gossip Game
Addressing Relational Bullying and Providing Support

Relational bullying happens when a group builds its identity by keeping an individual out and attacking this person's reputation, value, and other relationships. Sometimes the group also taunts the excluded person. At other times the group acts as if that person is not there. Usually one person leads the shunning process, but others in the group actively participate or passively let it happen.

My Own Story

Martha was the bane of my childhood. From the time I was seven until I was ten, I'd go to school dreading recess. All the girls would run to play the wonderful games that Martha would lead. With all my heart, I wished we could be friends.

If I tried to join in a game, Martha would call the other girls away from me, saying, "You don't want to play with that little brat. You might get her cooties." She and her friends would whisper words like 'ugly' about my dark, curly hair and olive skin, point at me, giggle, and turn their backs.

Asking my parents or teachers for help simply never occurred to me. Away from the cluster of girls, I'd sit alone by the locked door of the classroom and read a book, escaping into the world of my imagination and waiting for recess to be over. I suffered through recess each morning, lunchtime, and afternoon day after day after day for over three long years.

One day in the fifth grade, Martha and her followers trapped me in the bathroom. When I tried to slip past them to get out the door, Martha shoved me backwards, knocking me down. Pushed beyond endurance after years of being left out and ridiculed, I got up silently and kicked her hard in the shins. As I left the bathroom, Martha started crying and screamed, "You'll get in trouble for this. I'm telling on you."

Martha and the other girls went running to the teacher, claiming that I had kicked Martha and that she hadn't done anything at all. To her eternal credit, my teacher believed me over the word of the other girls. From my adult perspective, I can imagine that she must have observed the playground situation, even though the policy at that time in my school was that adults were not to interfere.

Over fifty years later, I can still remember being a terrified, shy ten-year-old who never got into trouble at school, feeling sick to my stomach when the teacher asked to speak with me alone. To this day, I can remember the kindness in her voice. "Speaking unofficially, Irene," my teacher said, "Good for you! Officially, please do your best not to let this happen again."

After that, to my astonishment, Martha started trying to get me into her group. At first, I thought I was in heaven. Having her acting so nice to me felt so wonderful.

Suddenly, I realized that Martha was starting to pick on another girl whose family did not have much money. As this girl stood there alone, looking sad, Martha and her followers laughed at her clothes. Martha nudged my arm to get me to join in.

I wanted so badly to be part of their group, but a dawning sense of justice told me that I simply couldn't do to this other girl what had been done to me. Gathering all the courage I had, I walked away from the group I had longed for years to belong to and went to talk to the girl they were harassing.

After that, Martha and I stayed away from each other. Some of the girls in her group eventually ended up becoming my friends.

Relational Bullying

Much of Martha's behavior was a form of what is now called "relational aggression" or "relational bullying." This term refers to the use of social networks to be hurtful to someone by spreading gossip, encouraging exclusion, and using other covert forms of personal attack.

In his profound book, *A Different Drum: Community Making and Peace*, author M. Scott Peck, M.D., describes how unhealthy groups can create a sense of purpose and value for themselves by choosing another group or an individual to be a common enemy.

This behavior is not new. In some cultures, both now and in the past, the most severe punishment anyone can receive is shunning. The experience of being banned from the community can have damaging and even deadly consequences.

Too often, relational aggression between young people is not taken that seriously by many adults. They will make suggestions that usually don't work very well, such as, ""Just ignore them and play with someone else."

Increasing evidence shows that being shunned can be devastating for a child. Children can internalize the message from their peers that they are "losers"

> *A child who is the target of relational aggression needs adult help.*

and act in self-destructive ways. Some children have become very depressed or even committed suicide. Some have become bitter and dealt with their hurt in very aggressive ways.

A child who is the target of relational aggression needs adult help. This behavior is hard to confront directly, and regular boundary-setting skills usually aren't enough to stop it. Without support, a child may start to believe that everyone important in the world thinks he or she is worthless.

Minimizing the pain of this experience is a mistake. Adults can often step in with younger children. An older child needs an adult to provide support, but not take over. Adults can provide support by listening to children's feelings with compassion and without lecturing and by coaching them to practice skills that can address the problem.

Adjusting Emotional Distance

When others are being unkind, children and adults can learn a variety of ways for protecting their emotional safety. As described above, in Kidpower, we teach our students how to throw hurting words away into their personal Trash Cans and recycle them into affirmations. We also teach how to screen out hurtful comments, gestures, and grimaces while taking in useful information.

For dealing with important people who go back and forth between being great to being rude, we teach how to Adjust Your Emotional Distance as a useful tool for enjoying the good in the relationship while protecting yourself from what is upsetting.

"Libby and I were best friends since we were little kids," ten-year-old Marisa mourned. "But now Libby acts so mean to me. She doesn't want me to spend time with anybody except her, and she says that I am a bad friend when I do. Sometimes, Libby tries to get other girls to stay away from me and play only with her. I don't want to lose Libby's friendship, because sometimes she can be very fun, but I don't know what to do."

"A friend who starts acting like a bully can cause a lot of hurt," I said sympathetically. "People often wonder what they did wrong and feel betrayed."

Marisa nodded her head sadly.

"This is hard to do at first, but you can learn to change your emotional distance from Libby, instead of keeping your heart completely open to her all the time," I suggested. "That way, when your friend is acting in a way that is emotionally safe, you can be emotionally open. When she is acting in a way that is emotionally unsafe, you can protect your heart by being emotionally further away from her."

I showed Marisa what I meant by using a physical example. First, I pretended to be Libby in a good mood. We stood close and gave each other a hug. Next, I started to be rude, saying, "Why didn't you come over to my house yesterday after school?" I coached Marisa to step away from me each time I was rude, so that her physical distance matched her emotional distance.

When others are being unkind, children and adults can learn a variety of ways for protecting their emotional safety.

Pretending to be Libby, I got progressively ruder, saying, "You are such a bad friend!" "I never liked you anyway. I just hung out with you out of pity." "You are just useless!" Marisa kept moving back, until she realized that she was ready to leave completely.

I acknowledged that Marisa might lose this friendship if Libby's behavior continued, but that this was not something that Marisa could control. It would be sad if this happened, but it would not be her fault.

The "I'd Like to Join the Game" Practice

Another way that kids pick on other kids is by not letting them play games. The rule at many schools is that everybody gets a turn or that everybody gets a chance to play. But, teachers usually tell kids who are getting left out to try to work it out themselves.

In one second-grade class, I asked the students what sorts of things kids said to stop other kids from joining a game. This led to quite a lively discussion with many examples. We then brainstormed answers for these reasons for exclusion.

Reason: "You're not good enough."
Response: "I'll get better if I practice."

Reason: "You're too good and nobody else gets a chance."
Response: "I just want to play. I'll agree to rotate so that everybody will have a turn."

Reason: "Only people wearing yellow can play this game."
Response: "Since green is a mixture of yellow and blue, this green shirt actually has yellow in it."

Reason: "You cheat."
Response: "I didn't mean to. Let's make sure we agree on the rules ahead of time."

Reason: "There are too many here already."
Response: "There's always room for one more."

Reason: "You had to have watched the show on TV last night to play."
Response: "I'll use my imagination. Just tell me what the rules are."

In workshops, we give students the chance to practice being persistent in asking to be included and being an advocate for another student. We remind them that staying cheerful and assertive works much better than acting whiny or irritated.

Our instructor Marc asks Daniel and Roxanne, who are both eight years old and who have done this before, to help him demonstrate. He sets the stage by explaining, "Let's imagine that I am a kid at your school. Roxanne and I are playing catch, and Daniel wants to play."

As Marc and Roxanne pretend to toss a ball back and forth, Daniel approaches them. "I'd like to join the game," he says cheerfully and confidently. Marc pretends to be a bully and says in a nasty voice, "No way! You always spoil everything by dropping the ball."

Daniel stays calm and says firmly, "I'll get better if I practice. I really want to play." (He imagines throwing Marc's words into his personal trash can.)

Marc says meanly, "I said that you're not good enough. Go away."

Roxanne, who has been watching up until now, speaks up. "That was a hurtful thing to say. Give him a chance," she tells Marc.

"But he drops the ball," Marc complains. "And he takes so long to get it."

Both Daniel and Roxanne speak up together saying, "We don't feel good leaving anybody out. Anyway, the rule at our school is that everybody gets to play."

Marc pretends to be angry and says, "I won't play if Daniel does."

Roxanne says calmly, "I'm sad that you feel that way. I hope that you'll change your mind." She and Daniel start tossing their imaginary ball.

Marc then gives each student the chance to practice being both the kid who wants to play and the kid who speaks up. Each student chooses which form of exclusion he or she wants to practice dealing with.

The Meet-New-People Personal Safety Tactic
In the sixth grade of a small private elementary school, the students were nervous about having to start at a new, much bigger school the following year. Each of these eleven-year-old children said that their biggest fear was of being alone.

We decided to turn this problem into a practice by having each student imagine being alone at the new school. The student approached a group of students who acted like they knew each other and said cheerfully and confidently, "Hello, I'm new here. What's your name?"

Sometimes the students in the group pretended to be friendly right away. Sometimes they acted annoyed or ignored the person practicing. We coached each student to find someone who was sitting all alone to approach and introduce her or himself.

The Gossip Game
Talking about what is happening in people's lives is interesting, but passing on unkind gossip is hurtful and can be damaging to their reputation. The Gossip Game is a fun way to practice changing negative messages to positive ones and to show how each person has the power to change negative gossip.

This is somewhat like the game of Telephone where one person whispers a sentence in the ear of another who whispers it to the next until, after several people have done this, you find that the original sentence has completely changed.

In the Gossip Game, you say the sentence out loud and you make it be unkind gossip about someone who is NOT a real person. For example, "I heard that X thinks that Y is really dumb."

A possible reply might be, "Y seems smart to me! X seems nice, too. I'll believe that she says mean things when I hear her myself."

You go around the circle taking turns giving negative messages and then finding ways to make them positive.

Compliments Practice

Children benefit from practice in giving compliments generously and receiving compliments graciously. Have a regular compliments time on a daily, weekly, or monthly basis in your family, day care, youth group, or school. Adults need to lead to ensure that everyone gets complimented an equal amount, that each person says something nice to each other person, and that the receiver responds appreciatively.

Make sure that compliments are genuine and do not contain an insult in the giver's tone of voice, facial expressions, or choice of words. Teach children to give compliments about something other than what people look like, such as about what they do or how they act. For example, "You know how to listen. You make funny jokes. You are fun to play with. You are a good helper."

Taking in compliments.

Addressing Relational Bullying and Providing Support

Ten ways adults can help children:

1   Listen with compassion. Seek professional counseling if the child continues to be upset.

2   Give the child opportunities to develop new relationships by getting involved with social groups away from school and activities to support their sense of worth.

3   Get the school to teach about relational aggression. The Internet contains a great deal of excellent information. See relationalaggression.com for a list of resources .

4   Have specific school rules about exclusion and a clear procedure that everyone knows to follow when it happens.

5   Ask all students to make written contracts not to gossip, exclude, or badmouth others.

6   Encourage children to write their experiences and feelings down. Journaling can help relieve pain and increase awareness. Documenting the problem in writing helps to define what is going on and can be a tool to get the attention of the adults in charge.

7   Acknowledge the temptation to gossip, because people's lives are interesting and because it is a way of sharing. Follow-up by explaining how gossiping about someone can become damaging when it hurts the reputation of this person.

8   Teach young people how to act confident, be assertive, protect their feelings, adjust their emotional distance, meet new people, be persistent in asking to be included, and be persistent in getting help. Give them the chance to practice staying assertive and confident while being rejected, assessing when it is time to go away, and finding someone else to talk with.

9   Educate young people about the importance of being an advocate instead of a witness. Give young people the chance to practice out loud the words to say in order to speak up respectfully and powerfully, as well as how to leave and get help.

10   Stay aware that there might be more than one side to the story. Jumping in and taking sides is often not as useful as guiding young people to find their own solutions.

Chapter Eleven

Being Brave to Set Boundaries and Advocate for Others

Setting boundaries with puppets.

Setting Boundaries With Duck
Speaking Up About Putdowns
Walking Our Talk
Balance of Power
Speaking Up to Stop Prejudice
Preparing Young People to be Brave to Stop Bullying

Speaking up takes courage. Speaking up takes the skills of knowing the words to say and how to deal with negative reactions. Finally, speaking up takes wisdom, because at times, speaking up is a mistake. What if a dangerous person is insulting you or others at a time when no adult authority figure is around to keep the situation from escalating? In such situations, the best plan is to leave and get help, which is also a form of taking action.

Setting Boundaries With Duck

One form of bullying is to mimic someone in a way that is demeaning. Having others make insulting caricatures of your speech, tone, words, posture, and gestures can be a huge trigger.

Even very young children will recognize this. In Head Start classes, we use the following demonstration with three-year-olds and a puppet. In the following example, the child is Laurie and the puppet is Duck.

Duck tugs Laurie's hair gently with its wings and looks naughty.

Laurie sets a boundary by removing Duck's wings from her hair and saying, "Please stop."

Duck mimics Laurie's words and tone in a way that is clearly intended to make fun of her, "Please stop. Na! Na! Na!"

All the preschool children gasp along with Laurie. "What's that called?" I ask.

"Copying," they all say. "That's not nice!"

Laurie looks worried and a bit stuck, so I coach her, "When people are rude, you can be brave and speak up. You can say to Duck, 'That's not funny!'"

Immediately, Laurie pushes Ducks' wings away and says, "Please stop. That's not funny."

Again Duck copies rudely, "Please stop. That's not funny. Sppppttt."

Laurie tries again, "Copying is not funny. I said stop. I don't like it."

To the fascination of my young audience at such amazing badness, Duck copies Laurie again. Duck repeats everything she says over and over, adding obnoxious noises and fluttering around her head.

I ask Laurie, "Do you feel like being mean back to Duck?"

As she nods her head, I add, "You are being very brave to stay in charge of your body. Now, use your Mouth Closed Power, your Walk Away Power, and your Getting Help Power."

Laurie squeezes her lips shut, walks away with awareness, and tells her teacher, "Duck is copying me. I said stop. Duck's not listening. I need help."

Her proud teacher puts her arm around Laurie and says, "You did a good job. I will talk to Duck!"

Speaking Up About Putdowns
Whether a putdown is directed toward them or at someone else, young people need to understand that stopping putdowns with their family, friends, and classmates is like stopping pollution or littering. Stopping putdowns might not always be possible, but trying when they can is important, especially with their peers.

Common putdowns include laughing, making rude gestures or sounds, mimicking, and saying insulting things to make someone feel embarrassed, uncomfortable, or ashamed. Putdowns also include making negative remarks about someone behind her or his back for the purpose of getting others to think less of this person. This is different than speaking up about a problem to get help, because the purpose is not to find a solution, but to be hurtful.

Depending on the nature of the putdown and the age of our students, verbal responses that we might have young people practice include:

• That's not funny. Please stop.
• That's a mean thing to say. I don't like it.
• That's not cool.
• What purpose does it serve to say that? It sounds like an insult.
• That's disrespectful. Please stop."
• That's prejudice. That's not acceptable to me.
• That's a mean thing to do. Stop or I'll leave.
• That's bullying. We promised not to do that, and I want to keep our promises.
• That's dishonorable. You are a better person than that.

We also help young people come up with "I" statements such as, "I feel sad when you say unkind things about people. Please stop."

Speak up and advocating for yourself and others takes both courage and wisdom.

Most people don't like being told what to do, which is why we prepare our students to persist when they speak up. We have them practice out loud finding positive, non-attacking responses to these common negative reactions.:

1. The Sense of Humor Reaction
Negative Comment: Can't you take a joke?
Possible Response: That was unkind. Being hurtful to people is not funny to me.

2. The Belittling Reaction
Negative Comment: You're overreacting. You're oversensitive.
Possible Response: Perhaps. All the same, I feel uncomfortable when you make comments like that. Let's talk about something else instead.

3. The Innocent Reaction
Negative Comment: But he/she is not even here. So what does it matter?
Possible Response: It makes people think less of him/her. Being mean behind someone's back does not make it less mean.

4. The Being Factual Reaction
Negative Comment: I was just stating my honest opinion. It's a free country.
Possible Response: If someone used words like that about you, my honest opinion is that you would feel attacked.

5. The Being Helpful Reaction
Negative Comment: I was just trying to be helpful. Can't you handle the truth?
Possible Response: When you put down something that a person cannot change, it is not helpful. When you use rude words to tell me you don't like something that I might or might not decide to change, that is not helpful.

6. The Blaming Reaction
Negative Comment: It's your fault. I had to say this because youmade me mad.
Possible Response: If you say rude things, this is your responsibility. It is not anyone's fault but your own. You can explain why you are unhappy another time.

7. The Changing the Subject Reaction
Negative Comment: You are really wrong because you _____ (a completely unrelated complaint).
Possible Response: You are changing the subject. You can complain about what I did later, but right now I want you to stop saying mean things.

8. The Threatening Reaction
Negative Comment: I'll make you sorry that you said that.
Possible Response: Stop or I'll leave. Stop or I'll tell. (Or just leaving and getting help without saying anything further to this person.)

9. The Denial Reaction
Negative Comment: I never said that. That's not what I meant.
Possible Response: **Option 1** (If there is any possibility you are wrong):

If we want children to use respectful communication, we must do so ourselves.

If that's true, then I apologize for believing you'd say something so awful.

Option 2 (If this is something that happens repeatedly): I have a different memory about this than you do. So, does this mean that you agree that that would be an awful thing to say?

Walking Our Talk

Like me, you might recognize yourself as well as other people in some of these defensive reactions. Respectful communication takes hard work from everyone involved.

As one teacher said, "A girl in my class was constantly harassing other kids by making devastating comments about everything they did. We discovered that she was copying how her parents joked with each other at home."

If we want to stop young people from using putdowns, we must stop making putdowns ourselves. Even if we didn't have any intention to be insulting, adults provide an important role model when we show children that we can listen respectfully any time someone feels insulted by our actions or words. We don't have to agree, but we do need to show that we are willing to understand other points of view.

No matter what our intentions were, if someone was insulted or hurt by something we said or did, we can say, "I am sorry for saying this in a way that was hurtful." If we were wrong, we can say, "I was wrong. That was a thoughtless thing for me to say. I am sorry." If we were expressing a valid concern, we can say, "I did not mean to hurt your feelings, but I do need to tell you about this problem. Is there a way that I can say it that you will not find insulting?"

Seeing adults do this is tremendously educational for their children.

Adults can tell children as soon as they are old enough to understand, "None of us is perfect, and we all make mistakes. When someone does not like something that you say or do, feeling unhappy about this is normal. Instead of saying something back right away, you can learn to get centered and to listen. Try to ask questions until you can understand why the other person is unhappy with you. Even if you don't agree, you can say that you are sorry for hurting someone's feelings."

Balance of Power

In workshops with older children and teens, we sometimes demonstrate what happens when people decide not to come to the defense of the victim but stand by and watch as a person bullies someone else.

Our instructors Antonie and Ryan recruit some students to help in the demonstration. Ryan has the students stand behind him as he points at Antonie. He tells them, "Imagine that I am your age. My pointing at Antonie like this is not realistic. My pointing represents the many different ways that I might be bullying her by calling her names, giving her the silent treatment, making threats, or making fun of her."

Everyone watches as Ryan points at Antonie. He has the group behind him and she is standing alone.

"How do you suppose Antonie feels right now?" Ryan asks everyone.

Most students give the same answers: Sad. Alone. Afraid.

"And," Ryan continues, "how do you suppose I feel?"

"Powerful," the students say. "Like you have all the control. Proud."

Finally, Ryan waves towards the young people behind him. "How do they feel?" he asks.

"Part of the group," the students say. "Safe. But not too safe, because your pointing at her could turn towards them. Sorry, but glad that it's not happening to them."

Ryan asks, "Would being the first person to go over and support Antonie be hard to do?"

"Yes," the students say. They watch as the first one of the group and then another goes over to stand next to Antonie.

Next, Ryan helps build understanding by asking leading questions. "Does it get easier when you are not the first? 'Yes.' How does Antonie feel now? 'Better.' How do I feel? 'Less sure of yourself.' How do these kids still behind me feel? 'Like going over, too.'"

The kids behind Ryan continue to walk over to Antonie until he is the one who is standing alone, still pointing at Antonie. "Notice," he explains, "That my behavior hasn't changed at all, but the situation has changed completely. How does Antonie feel now?"

"Good," the students say. "Like she belongs."

Ryan gestures to the group behind Antonie and asks them directly, "How do you feel?"

Almost always, one or more of the group behind Antonie will raise their arms and start pointing back at Ryan.

"This is very interesting," Ryan says. "If you wanted to support Antonie because you thought that my pointing at her was wrong, it is just repeating the same pattern of bullying if you start pointing back. Instead, you want to support Antonie. You could say, 'That was really hard.' Or, 'I'm sorry that happened to you.' You could put a hand on her shoulder. You could ask a teacher or another adult for help. It is safest for everyone if you can support Antonie without acting in an attacking way yourself."

As the students lower their arms and move closer to Antonie, Ryan asks one last question. "How do you think I feel now, with no one behind me?"

It is important for adults to let children know, "none of us is perfect, and we all make mistakes, and we can say we are sorry when we hurt someone's feelings."

The students say, "Alone. Powerless. Left out."

"In fact," Ryan smiles as he walks over to the group with Antonie. "I might get tired of being here by myself pointing and decide to join these kids to do something else instead. It would be fine for me to join this group as long as I didn't do any of the bullying behavior I was doing before."

Antonie then points out that, if someone has been bullying, your plan can be to say "yes" with a boundary.

In his role as the former bully, Ryan comes up to the group and says, "Can I play?"

"Yes," Antonie says calmly and confidently, "But no pushing!"

In workshops, we then have students practice this in small groups, so that they each can feel what it is like to be the person pointing, the person being pointed at, and the bystanders — and how shifts in the balance of power change your feelings in each role.

Speaking Up to Stop Prejudice
Not a Perfect World
In a perfect world, no one would care if people were different, as long as they weren't being hurtful to anyone.

In a perfect world, people would not be bothered or harmed by others because they are of different religions, races, sexual orientations or identities, appearances, incomes, or cultures.

In a perfect world, people would not be bothered or harmed by others because they are of different religions, races, sexual orientations or identities, appearances, incomes, or cultures. Different colors of skin and shapes of faces and bodies would be celebrated rather than judged. Whether children have married parents, divorced parents, two moms, two dads, or foster parents would not matter. If children's families have problems, this would not be a reason for other people to think less of them.

But I don't have to tell you that this is not a perfect world. Prejudice because of differences can lead to bullying and cruel teasing, which results in misery and even suicide due to young people feeling alone and desperate.

One of the ways to make our world safer for everyone is to speak up against prejudice and injustice. Just witnessing or even going along with bullying and putdowns without saying or doing anything means that prejudice and injustice will continue.

Thinking First Before Speaking Up
Choosing when and how to intervene is essential in order to do speak up safely. Sometimes the wisest and most effective choice is to leave and get help.

In our workshops with older children and teens, we explain, "Before you speak up, you want to think first. Is this a group of friends being thoughtless, or someone I don't know acting tough on the street? If someone you don't know is making prejudiced remarks, the safest plan is almost always to walk away and get to a place where someone can help you.

"But if someone you do know, maybe at work or at school, is making putdown comments and jokes, you can make the choice to speak up. Speaking up against prejudice can be powerful, but takes courage. Be prepared to persist because people are likely to be mad at you at first or go into denial."

Too often, people will tolerate prejudice when it is delivered in the form of a joke. Unfortunately, promoting prejudice through humor also promotes injustice.

Most people are clear that some kinds of jokes are destructive, but they will laugh at other jokes that are equally prejudicial. For example, someone might find jokes about race totally out of bounds, but think that jokes about sexual orientation or appearances are really funny.

Role Plays for Older Children, Teens, and Adults

In Teenpower and Fullpower workshops where this has been requested, we often use role-plays so students can practice dealing with negative comments relating to size, gender, sexuality, religion, race, ethnicity, ability, and other aspects of personal identity.

In each case, the adult leading the practice plays the role of a friend who is making prejudicial remarks. We give students the opportunity to come up with their own examples and coach them if they get stuck on the words to say. We remind them to stay assertive rather than becoming passive or aggressive.

1. *Body Size* Role-Play

First, the instructor sets the stage by saying, "Suppose you and I are friends, sitting outside on a bench during school."

Next, the instructor makes prejudiced remarks in a sneering voice like, "Hey look! ... That guy is so *fat*! ... He needs two seats on the bus!" Or, "Have you seen that girl in sixth grade? She's so skinny you can't see her! ... She's probably stupid too."

The student says assertively, "I feel uncomfortable when you use somebody's size as a putdown. Please stop!" Or, "That sounds like prejudice and I don't want to hear it!"

The instructor pretends to act upset and says, "Can't you take a joke?" The student responds assertively, "I don't think prejudice is funny." Or, "That kind of joke isn't funny to me."

2. *Homophobia* Role-Play

First, the instructor sets the stage by saying, "Let's imagine that we are kids the same age at school. I am talking about someone on the other side of the room, and he or she can't hear us." Next, the instructor whispers in a mocking voice, pointing to an imaginary person in an empty spot on the other side of the room, "Yuck, look at that new girl! She looks like a boy. I bet she's a dyke." Or, "You see that guy? I heard he's a fag. Don't you just want to puke?"

The student says assertively, "Lots of great people are lesbians (or gay)!

Choosing when and how to intervene is essential. Sometimes the wisest and most effective choice is to leave and get help.

We all need to advocate for ourselves and for others.

I feel uncomfortable when you use that as a putdown. Please stop!" Or, "That sounds like a prejudiced remark, and I don't like that kind of talk!"

The instructor acts irritated and snaps, "Can't you take a joke?" Or, "Are you gay, too?"

The student responds calmly, "If I were gay, I'd be proud of it." Or, "My sexual identity is none of your business." She or he then adds, "I don't think prejudice is funny." Or, "This kind of joke isn't funny to me."

3. *Mean Jokes* Role-Play
First, the adult sets the stage by saying, "Suppose that we are with a group of friends and I start making mean jokes." Next, the adult laughs, "Have you heard that joke about the fatso that ate too much?! Or, "Did you hear that great joke about two stupid faggots? Ha! Ha! Ha!!" Or, while pulling the eyes sideways saying, "Look, I can make my eyes like a Chinaman." Or, mimicking someone's accent or behavior.

The student speaks up and says, "I feel uncomfortable when you joke about somebody's size (or sexual identity, looks, or accent) and use it as a putdown. Please stop!" Or, "That sounds like prejudice, and it upsets me!"

The adult pretends to be upset and reacts by saying, "But you joke like that all the time!"

The student responds by saying, "I used to joke like that until I realized how cruel it is. I don't want to be acting like a prejudiced person."

4. *Sexism* Role-Play
First the adult sets the stage by saying, "Let's imagine that we are students and we are talking about a girl who is not in class today." Next the adult says in a disgusted voice, "She must be a slut and sleep around to be so popular (get good grades/get ahead)."

The student responds, "Please stop. That sounds like prejudice and I don't want to hear it!"

The adult mimics in an irritating tone, "That sounds like prejudice and I don't want to hear it." With a disgusted face, the adult adds, "Well, I don't want to hear you going on and on about this. You're no fun to be with anymore!"

The student says, "I am sad that you feel that way because I like you a lot. There are lots of other great things we can talk about instead of putting people down. Wasn't the game (or movie) great last night?"

5. *Racism* Role-Play
First, the adult sets the stage by saying, "Let's imagine that we are kids the same age having lunch at school."

Next the adult starts making racist remarks, perhaps by quoting someone else as an authority, "You know what, my parents were talking about a study that says that Black people are just not as intelligent as White people. That's why they have so many problems. And there was another study that shows that those Mexicans are taking everyone's jobs."

The student says assertively, "I feel upset when you use a study or quote someone else to make a prejudiced remark."

The adult pretends to be reasonable and says, "But it was a scientific study. You can't argue with science."

The student responds assertively and says, "What we think is scientifically accurate changes all the time and contradicts itself. Other studies show that people are equally intelligent regardless of race and that there is great benefit to our society from our immigrants. I feel uncomfortable when you repeat negative remarks about groups of people. Please stop."

From Feeling Helpless to Feeling Empowered

These are only a few of the practices that are possible. Use examples that are relevant to the individuals doing the role-play. Let them tell you what language, gestures, expressions, and reactions are most likely. Find assertive, non-attacking responses for them to use in speaking up. Remind them that leaving and getting help can often be the most effective way to take action.

People of all ages are often silent in the face of prejudice because they don't know the words to say - and are afraid of the consequences. Being prepared by having thought through and practiced different responses can be the difference between someone feeling helpless and feeling empowered.

Preparing Young People to be Brave to Stop Bullying

1 Discuss what it feels like to know something is wrong and feel too afraid to speak up. Use stories from your own life when you can. Were there times when you didn't speak up about putdowns or other bullying and felt bad later? Were there times when you did speak up and it didn't work out so well? What did you learn?

2 Discuss times when people show courage by speaking up for themselves and others. This could be from books, movies, or activities like the Balance of Power exercise described above. Again, tell stories from your own life when you can and encourage children to tell their stories. Talk about what courage feels like "from the inside" to each person. How does it feel to do something that you know is right even if you are worried, scared, or uncomfortable about doing it?

3 At the age level that is appropriate, use the tactics above with examples from children's lives to let them practice speaking up about different kinds of putdowns. For younger children, this can be a great time to use a puppet to be the rude person so that you can easily coach.

4 For older children, let them decide ahead of time who the person creating the problem is, what the offensive words or actions are, what words they want to use to speak up, what defensive reaction they want to have to deal with, and what response they want to try. They can even write this up as a little script.

Chapter Twelve

Peer Pressure Tactics

Research shows that the biggest reason young people break the law is negative peer pressure.

Family Counselor and Author Sharon Scott
Positive and Negative Peer Pressure and Triggers
Using Tactics to Address Common Peer Problems
Preparing Young People to Deal With Peer Pressure

No matter how old or young we are, most of us want to be liked and respected by our peers. Especially as young people move into their pre-teen and teen years, the opinions of their peers often become much more important to them. To make wise decisions, they need to understand the role that peer pressure can play in influencing their choices and develop the skills to stand up to their peers when necessary.

Positive and Negative Peer Pressure and Triggers

In workshops, our instructor Jan defines peer pressure for her students by explaining, "Peers are people your age, and most of us want people our age to like us. Peer pressure happens when someone your age tries to get you to do something. Positive peer pressure helps you do your best, like people cheering at a game. With negative peer pressure, someone tries to persuade you to do something that might hurt someone, be dangerous, or get you into trouble."

Jan explains how managing triggers is a useful tool for managing peer pressure. "Being triggered means that you get so excited or so upset that you stop thinking clearly. When you are not thinking clearly, you are less likely to make wise choices for yourself. Negative triggers make you feel bad. A negative trigger might be wanting so badly not to be left out or thought less of by members of the group that you go along with the crowd. A positive trigger might happen when you get so caught up in doing something exciting that you forget to think about the consequences.

"Sometimes people do things when they get caught up in peer pressure that they would *never* do otherwise and feel bad about later," Jan continues. "Instead of getting triggered into making a poor decision, you can Get Centered and Think First."

Family Counselor and Author Sharon Scott

Thanks to permission from family counselor Sharon Scott, LPC, LMFT, author of the excellent book about peer pressure in the teen years, *How to Say No and Keep Your Friends* (HRD Press, 1997, 800-822-2801 http://www.hrdpress.com/SharonScott), we have incorporated some ideas from her peer pressure reversal skills program into our Kidpower program.

Sharon Scott formerly served as the director of the First Offender Program of the Dallas, Texas, police department, a program for adolescents who commit one to five offenses. She found that the biggest reason that young people broke the law was because of negative peer pressure. She had them practice her Peer Pressure Reversal skills and 79 percent were successful as measured by never being arrested again. She has a wide range of books and training for all ages about peer pressure and other topics including the parent guide, *Peer Pressure Reversal: An Adult Guide to Developing a Responsible Child.*

Using Tactics to Address Common Peer Problems

Using ideas from Sharon Scott's Peer Pressure Reversal Tactics, Jan then directs different students in acting out common problems that young people might face with peers.. She reminds students that they need to be cheerful or matter-of-fact, not sarcastic. Also, if a tactic doesn't work, the safest plan is to leave.

Students practice getting out of the following situations in ways that save face for the other person.

1. The *Cutting Class* Role-Play

Pedro and Bill pretend to be two friends waiting outside before school. Bill says, "Hey Pedro, that substitute is so stupid she'll never notice we're missing. Let's cut class. Come on! Hurry, before they..."

Pedro uses the tactic of Leaving. He interrupts Bill and says, "Gotta go, bye! He walks away cheerfully with a wave.

2. The *Putting Down Another Kid* Role-Play

Carol and Maggie pretend to be two friends sitting in the lunchroom at school.

Maggie points and says, "Hey, Carol, look at that new girl. She's really gross. Let's tell everyone to stay away from her."

Carol uses the tactic of Changing the Subject by saying, "Do you want to know what *she* said about *you*?" (Asking people if they want to know what someone else said about them is a very effective way of changing the subject.)

Maggie looks surprised and asks eagerly, "Yes! What did she say?"

Carol says cheerfully, "She says that you seem very nice."

Maggie looks taken aback.

3. The *Showing Off a Gun* Role-Play

Billy and Robert pretend to be two friends who are visiting Billy's house. Billy says, "Hey, my Dad just got a gun for protection. See, it's right here in this drawer."

Robert uses the tactic of Making an Excuse and says as he runs out the door, "*Oh no!* I forgot to feed my dog! Sorry, I gotta go!"

4. The *Talking in Class* Role-Play

Allie and Megan pretend to be two friends sitting next to each other in class. The teacher has warned that the next student who says anything will have to stay after school.

Instead of getting triggered into making a poor decision, you can get centered and Think First.

Megan pokes Allie and says, "Hey, Allie, guess what I heard at a party yesterday. Psst. Psst."

Allie uses the tactic of Ignoring and pretends to keep doing her schoolwork as Megan nudges and prods her, complaining, "What's *with* you!?"

5. The *Toilet Papering the Neighbor's House* Role-Play
Niko and Will pretend to be friends who are standing outside Will's house. Will says, "I'm really mad at my neighbor. He is so mean to me, and he's out of town. I know! Let's toilet-paper his house!"

Niko uses the tactic of Acting Shocked. He puts his hands to his face like the little boy in the movie *Home Alone* and says in a horrified voice, "Are you *crazy*? We'll be grounded *forever* if we do that!"

6. The *Using Drugs* Role-Play
Marjorie and Olivia pretend to be two friends who are really worn out studying for a test.

Olivia yawns and says, "I'm tired. I know someone who has some pills that will make us feel really good so we can concentrate. Why don't I call him to see if we can get some?"

Marjorie chooses the tactic of Using Flattery and says, "I like you too much to agree to use drugs with you. It's not worth the risk even if we fail the test. Let's do some stretches and see if that doesn't help."

7. The *Sneaking Out of the House* Role-Play
Jamie and Tom pretend to be best friends who are staying at Tom's house for an overnight.

Tom stretches and says, "I'm bored. Everyone is asleep. Let's sneak out of the house and go into the park. They'll never know."

Jamie uses the tactic of Having a Better Idea and says, "I have a better idea. Let's watch the movie we rented. We already paid for it!"

8. The *Stealing* Role-Play
Joe and Peter pretend to be two friends in the store.

Joe says, "Hey, Peter, you distract the cashier, and I'll steal some magazines."

Peter decides to use the tacking of Using Flattery and says, "I really like you, and I don't want to get us into trouble. It could ruin our friendship if we steal." Peter pays for his candy and quickly walks out of the store.

9. The *Prank Calls* Role-Play
Lila and Latisha are having a sleepover.

Lila says, "Hey, Latisha, lets make some prank calls. Let's order a bunch of pizzas for Juan." (Many young people are surprised to find out that prank calls are against the law.)

Latisha uses the strategy of Making a Joke by saying, "We can't. I've got phonophobia today." (Any joke, no matter how dumb, is okay as long as it doesn't put the other person down.)

Preparing Young People to Deal With Peer Pressure

1   Explain what peer pressure is. Tell stories of times from your own life when your friends supported you in doing your best and times when going along with friends got you into trouble or to do something you were sorry about later. Look for examples from books and movies of this happening.

2   Encourage young people to tell their own stories. Ask for times when their friends have supported them in ways that made their lives better and for times when friends have gotten them to do things that made their lives worse.

3   Explain about how being triggered positively or negatively by peers can cause problems.

4   Read Sharon Scott's books (www.hrdpress.com/SharonScott) for children and for adults. Using her Peer Pressure Reversal tactics, make up role-plays for situations that your children might encounter and practice them.

Chapter Thirteen
Preventing Sexual Harassment

The Problem –AAUW Study
Harassment-Free Schools and Work Places
Addressing Sexism and Homophobia
Dealing With Unwanted Sexual Attention
Actions to Help Prevent and Stop Sexual Harassment of Young People

As they get older, young people need boundaries about when and how to express their sexual feelings. They need to understand that having sexual feelings is normal, but showing them can be intrusive to others. They can feel one way and act another. Adults are responsible for providing excellent role models and for stopping inappropriate behavior in educational, youth group, or work settings, such as staring, making suggestive noises or comments, and any kind of sexual touching.

83% of girls and 79% of boys report having experienced sexual harassment.

The Problem – AAUW Study
In 2003, the American Association of University Women (AAUW) commissioned a study by Harris Interactive to survey a nationally representative group of 2,064 students ranging from twelve to eighteen years old about sexual harassment in their schools. This was a follow-up to a similar AAUW study done in 1993.

In the study, sexual harassment was defined as "unwanted and unwelcome sexual behavior that interferes with your life. Sexual harassment is not behaviors that you like or want (for example, wanted kissing, touching, or flirting)." "Non-physical harassment" was explained to mean unwanted sexual behavior that does not involve touching such as "taunting, rumors, graffiti, jokes or gestures." The study uses examples such as being spied on while showering or dressing.

The findings, reported in the AAUW publication, *Hostile Hallways: Bullying, Teasing, and Sexual Harassment in School*, indicate that:

• 83 percent of girls and 79 percent of boys report having experienced sexual harassment.

• For many students, sexual harassment is an ongoing experience: over one in four students experience it "often." These numbers do not differ by whether the school is urban, suburban, or rural.

• Peer-on-peer harassment is most common for both boys and girls, although seven percent of boys and girls experiencing physical or nonphysical harassment report being harassed by a teacher.

- Half of the boys reporting harassment have been non-physically harassed by a girl or woman, and 39 percent by a group of girls or women. In contrast, girls are most likely to report harassment by one boy or man (73 percent in non-physical harassment; 84 percent in physical harassment).

- 35 percent of students who have been harassed report that they first experienced it in elementary school.

- Most harassment occurs under teachers' noses in the classroom (61 percent for physical harassment and 56 percent for non-physical) and in the halls (71 percent for physical harassment and 64 percent for nonphysical).

- Students are perpetrators, too. Slightly more than half of the students (54 percent) say that they have sexually harassed someone else at some time while they were in school.

- Although large groups of both boys and girls report experiencing harassment, girls are more likely to report being negatively affected by it. Girls are far more likely than boys to feel "self-conscious" (44 percent for girls compared to 19 percent for boys), "embarrassed" (53 percent compared to 32 percent), and "less confident" (32 per-cent to 16 percent) due to an incident of harassment. Girls are more likely than boys to change behavior because of the experience, including not talking as much in class (30 percent to 18 percent) and avoiding the person who harassed them (56 percent to 24 percent).

Harassment-Free Schools and Work Places

In response to the above findings, the AAUW developed an excellent resource guide for students, parents, and educators titled, *Harassment-Free Hallways: How to Stop Sexual Harassment in Schools*. This free online publication provides surveys for students and staff, educational materials, and policy suggestions to help create a respectful, safe school environment. This guide helps to define the difference between flirting and hurting.

Sexual harassment is against the law in many countries, including the United States. The U.S. Department of Education's Office of Civil Rights publishes an on-line pamphlet titled, *Sexual Harassment: It's Not Academic*, that defines students' rights to a nondiscriminatory, safe learning environment and gives clear definitions of what is and is not considered sexual harassment.

Examples of sexual conduct might include: sexual advances; touching of a sexual nature; graffiti of a sexual nature; displaying or distributing sexually explicit drawings, pictures, or written materials; sexual gestures; sexual or "dirty" jokes; pressure for sexual favors; touching oneself sexually or talking about one's sexual activity in front of others; spreading rumors or rating other students as to sexual activity or performance; etc.

Sexual conduct must be unwelcome to be considered sexual harassment. However, a student might not speak up right away because of embarrassment, confusion, or fear of retaliation. A student might be very upset and uncomfortable, but not have the ability to complain. Invited or not, it is against the law for an adult to sexually approach a person under the

Sexual harassment is fed by sexism and homophobia.

age of eighteen. It is against the law for an employer or teacher to put sexual pressure on an employee or student or to create a hostile or uncomfortable environment in work or school settings.

Addressing Sexism and Homophobia

Sexual harassment is fed by sexism and homophobia. According to the Merriam-Webster Online Dictionary, sexism means: "1) prejudice or discrimination based on sex; especially, discrimination against women; 2) behavior, conditions, or attitudes that foster stereotypes of social roles based on sex." Homophobia means, "irrational fear of, aversion to, or discrimination against homosexuality or homosexuals."

Many young people routinely use gender stereotypes and homophobia to make each other miserable. Adults need to address these issues in the moment and through education.

The media is one of the most powerful influences on today's youth. The Media Awareness Network in Canada has a wealth of lesson plans for different grade levels on how to teach media awareness skills. In their section, "Gender Stereotypes and Sexual Assault," they have lessons that include asking what it means to "act like a man" and "be a lady," how this affects the students' images of themselves, and how this relates to sexual harassment and violence. They also have lessons on diversity and violence, including homophobia and racism.

To stop sexual harassment, adults need to set a good example and speak up about behavior that happens in front of them. If we don't say anything, it leads young people into believing that this is acceptable to us.
Once, I was visiting an elementary school, and a ten-year-old boy playing tag almost ran into me. His friends all laughed at him, "Hey, you run like a *girl*!" I peered at the group of boys over the top of my sunglasses. "I very much hope," I said sternly, "that you intended the statement 'you run like a girl' to be a compliment! Did you?"

The boys squirmed and admitted, "Uh, not exactly."

Without identifying the boys, I repeated the comment to their teacher. Indignantly, she described the running feats of some great women athletes. This class came up with a plan of noticing joking comments that were actually a form of prejudice and finding examples to prove that the stereotype was incorrect.

In another workshop with a youth group, the pre-teen boys and girls told me that they wanted to throw away the words "faggot" and "gay" and "dyke" because the worst possible insult was for anyone to think that they might be homosexuals.

I said, "I feel sad when people use prejudice as a way of insulting people and of joking. Even if something isn't true about you, denying this kind of insult becomes a way of making the prejudice get bigger. People used to do this about race and sometimes still do. They do it about size. They do it about looks. They do it about sexuality. Stopping this kind of behavior takes courage, especially because these comments are so much a part of our culture.

"Whether you realize it or not, people you know are likely to be hurt by jokes about sexual orientation and identity, even if they pretend that this doesn't bother them. People you know or someone they care about a lot might be gay, lesbian, bi-sexual, transgender, or not sure.

"If someone uses a prejudiced remark to try to put you down," I continued, "you could throw away their intention to attack you, and say something that is positive without attacking anybody else, like, 'I'm proud to be who I am.'" One boy named Dennis said, "But what if I'm not gay and somebody thinks I am if I say that?"

I smiled at Dennis for having the courage to ask and explained, "You would be in very good company. There are many wonderful people who are gay and lesbian. Anyway, does it really matter what someone else thinks? What matters is what *you* think. You have to think about what kind of person you want to be. Right?"

Dennis thought for a moment and then smiled back at me. "Call me a faggot," he said.

I pointed at him and sneered, "You *faggot*!"

Dennis put his hands up like a fence and said, "That's a prejudiced remark, and I'm proud to be who I am."

Dealing With Unwanted Sexual Attention

When setting a boundary with someone about inappropriate behavior, stay centered and clear about your purpose of getting the behavior to stop without attacking the other person. Many people do not realize that their behavior is making another person uncomfortable. They may respond defensively at first because being told to stop forces them to change. The most effective way to prevent getting caught up in someone else's negative reaction is to focus on what you want to see changed.

When possible, our goal is to empower young people to speak up for themselves in stopping sexual harassment. Because nonphysical harassment is sometimes harder to confront, we often introduce how to set boundaries with staring. Our instructor Greg explains what he's doing as he stares at Loretta, who keeps moving to different parts of the room, "Imagine that we are two students your age. I keep staring at Loretta. I stare at her in the classroom."

As Greg stares, Loretta glances at him out of the corner of her eye, makes an irritated face, and looks away.

Greg continues his explanation. "I stare at her in the lunchroom." Greg stares and Loretta sighs. She glances at him again and he is still staring. "I stare at her when she's reading in the school library," Greg says. "She just can't get away from my staring."

Loretta goes up to Greg and says, "Please stop staring at me. I don't like it."

Adults need to address the issues of gender stereotypes, racism and homophobia in the moment as well as through education.

"I'm not doing anything!" Greg says. "It's just your imagination." Greg pauses in the role-play, turns to the class, and asks, "Well, it's true that I'm not touching Loretta, but am I still bothering her?"

Students' heads nod. Most of them don't like being stared at either.

Continuing the role-play, Greg says, "I can look anywhere I want. It's a free country!"

Loretta says, "Yes it is. And I am free to tell you that I expect you, instead of staring at me, to look the other way. Bothering people like this is against the rules here at our school."

"Oh, all right!" Greg says in an irritated tone. He looks away.

Greg points out that there is nothing wrong with feeling that someone looks wonderful, but there is something wrong with making that person uncomfortable by staring, pointing, or making suggestive noises. If he hadn't stopped, then Loretta would have had the right to ask the teacher for help so that she could feel comfortable at school.

Getting adult help when adults are the ones causing the problem with young people is especially important. When my daughter Chantal was twelve, she was one of only four girls in her advanced math class. She complained because her math teacher kept looking at her in a leering way and making suggestive remarks.

After talking it over with her father and me, Chantal told her math teacher the next time he started this behavior, "I feel uncomfortable when you talk about how I look. Please don't do that."

Instead of respecting her boundary, her math teacher made fun of her. He increased his remarks and started making drawings with women's breasts on the blackboard.

Although she didn't like the idea, I persuaded my daughter that it was important for me to tell her teacher that what he was doing was not okay, not only for her sake, but for the three other girls in her class.

I made an appointment to meet the math teacher after school and said very respectfully, "I think you're an excellent teacher. You may not be aware of some things you're doing that make Chantal uncomfortable. I feel that your teasing remarks about how she looks are just not appropriate."

The math teacher, who was a large man, seemed to get bigger and bigger and redder and redder in the face as I was talking, until he exploded, "In my thirty-two years of teaching, no one has ever spoken to me like this!"

"Well," I said cheerfully, feeling thankful for all of my self-defense training, "after thirty-two years, it's probably about time."

"Get real!" he snapped. "Your daughter needs to stop being oversensitive when someone just makes a joke! Anyway, *who* are *you* to talk to *me* like this?"

I'm her *mother*, I thought, and the co-founder of Kidpower! But what I said in a firm, calm voice was, "There are probably women right now who are sitting in a therapist's office saying that they stopped studying math or other subjects important to them because of this kind of joke. And there are probably boys who are making girls' lives miserable by following your poor example. What you're doing is a form of sexual harassment, and I want you to stop. If need be, we can ask the school counselor to help us understand each other."

In the face of this adult version of "Stop or I'll tell," the math teacher deflated like a pricked balloon. "I'll do whatever you want! " he said. This math teacher then added plaintively, "But I feel bad because your daughter doesn't *like* me!"

I sighed. "She might if you'd stop teasing her! However, it's *not* her job to like you, and it's *not* your job to like her. It's *your* job to teach her math, and it's *her* job to learn it."

After that, the math teacher's behavior changed, and Chantal did well in the class.

To stop sexual harassment, adults need to set a good example with their own behavior and speak up about behavior that is in front of them.

Actions to Help Prevent and Stop Sexual Harassment of Young People

1 Check the policy at your children's schools about sexual harassment. Encourage middle and high schools to do the surveys and follow the policy recommendations of the AAUW or another resource.

2 Make sure that pre-teens and teens know what kinds of behavior are considered sexual harassment.

3 Make it clear that you do not consider this behavior to be acceptable and that you want to know if it happens to them or to other kids in their school or youth group. Avoid laughing at sexist or homophobic jokes. Intervene to stop sexual harassment instead of overlooking it. Make sure that young people know that they have the right to be treated with respect and the responsibility to treat others with respect.

4 Ask young people to notice when sexist or homophobic language or images are used in the media, in conversations, in activities, and in books. Help them find people who don't fit these negative stereotypes.

5 Help young people become informed consumers of the media. Ask schools to provide media education or use these resources yourself.

6 As they start to become interested in each other sexually, ask young people to tell you what kinds of attention are welcome and what are unwelcome. Remind them that they have the right to *feel* any way they want, and that they have the responsibility to *act* in a way that is respectful to other people.

7 Give young people the opportunity to practice Boundary-Setting and Advocacy skills in the context of sexual harassment.

8 When young people are unable to solve problems for themselves, listen to the whole story, brainstorm solutions, and make a plan of action. If the sexual harassment does not stop, intervene with the adults who are supervising.

Chapter Fourteen

Other Solutions to Problems With Peers

Keep Working on It
Double-Check for Assertiveness
Leave
Find Safe Friends
Know Your Choices
Write Things Down
Figuring out Different Solutions to Bullying Problems

At Kidpower, we believe that everyone, adults and young people, have the right and responsibility to work towards creating cultures of caring, respect, and safety for all. Problems of indifference, unkindness, disrespect, and lack of safety won't go away overnight, but they aren't likely to change if we don't all keep working together to make things better.

As adults, we want the young people in our lives to tell us when they have problems. We want to empower them to find their own solutions when possible. We want to back them up. Even if we aren't able to find a good solution right away, young people are likely to feel much better knowing that their adults are on their side. We want them to know that we are doing our best and not quitting. The bottom line is that, if one solution doesn't work, we'll try another!

Double-Check for Assertiveness
"People Safety" skills are far more effective if they are used in an assertive way. If our students tell us that they tried these skills and it didn't work, we say, "Please show me exactly what you are doing. Let's act it out. Maybe we forgot to tell you something."

Most of the time, as soon as students show us what they are doing instead of just telling us, we can see immediately what the problem is. Their words aren't clear, even if they think they are. Their manner is either apologetic or rude, without their realizing it. Their body language is hesitant, although they might think they are being firm.

Of course, we are as encouraging as possible. "You are doing almost everything right, but this is like an electric circuit. If there is even a small place anywhere along the wire that is not connected, the electricity won't flow." We model what exact changes will increase assertiveness and then give students the chance to practice again.

Leave
Sometimes the only solution is to leave. Perhaps a specific school or

We believe that everyone, adults and young people, have the right and the responsibility to work towards creating cultures of caring, respect, and safety for all.

youth group lacks the adult support needed to make a commitment to solve problems. Perhaps a social dynamic has become too tough to solve. Changing schools or ending unsafe relationships is a form of target denial.

Often, young people don't like change, even if this means exchanging a bad situation for a potentially much better one. Kids get attached to what is familiar, and they often care about unsafe people. They may need support in getting more information about the pros and cons of different choices. They may need permission to grieve about the losses that come from leaving. They may need adults to make the choices for them.

"When she was in the third grade, we decided that Carmen needed to go to a different school mid-year," Carmen's parents said. "She was being bullied constantly, and her classroom was completely out of control. At first, Carmen didn't want to go, even though she was miserable.

"We told Carmen that it was okay to be sad about leaving her old school, and adjusting to the new one would take time. Finally, we took her to visit the new school. We asked her to tell us if there was anything we could do to make this change easier. Carmen said that she wanted to have a tee shirt with her new school's name on it, like some of the other kids had. We believe that, hard as it was, changing schools was one of the best decisions we made for our daughter's well-being."

Find Safe Friends
Having safe friends is one of the best protections against bullying. Learning how to judge when a friend is safe or unsafe is a major life skill.

The Kidpower office often gets poignant e-mail messages from young people from all over the world who are feeling very alone because of problems with friends. Their perception is that their parents are not available because they are too busy, sick, using drugs or alcohol, or in new romantic relationships and that their teachers don't care. They think that their friends are all they have, and their friends are being hurtful.

Below is a typical message and our reply about how to find adult help and how to tell the difference between safe and unsafe friends.

E-Mail Message: I am eleven and live in London. My friends say that I'm ugly and dumb and that I'm lucky they let me hang out with them. They boss me around all the time. If we go to the snack bar, I am always the one who pays for everybody and I don't have much money. My mum works really hard and is always so tired that I don't want to bother her. What should I do?

Kidpower Reply: This sounds really hard. Even if your mum is busy, she probably really does want to know what is going on with you. Try finding a time to tell her when she is rested up. Make sure that you really have her attention and ask her to please just listen until you can tell her the whole story.

Try thinking of other safe adults you could tell. Maybe there is a teacher at your school who you liked before, even if you are in a different class now. Maybe you have an adult family member who you could call. Think

Children may need adults to make choices for them.

of as many adults as possible that you believe act safely and respectfully – neighbors, counselors, youth group leaders, ministers, priests, rabbis, your coach in sports, or the parents of a friend. Finding the right adult to talk to can help you feel less alone and figure out what to do.

Sometimes kids who seem really cool and who do fun things are also mean or disrespectful to you. They might put you down, order you around, try to keep you from being friends with others, borrow money and never pay it back, expect you to pay for everything, want to have things only their way, make up stories about you, tell your secrets to everybody, and try to get you to do things that will get you into trouble.

Safe friends are kind, make plans with you, encourage other friendships, treat you with respect, pay back any money they owe, pay for their share of what things cost, do their share of the work, and encourage you to do things that are good for everyone. Safe friends respect your privacy unless anything unsafe is going on, in which case, they will help you find help.

If your friends say and do things that are hurtful, embarrassing, or disrespectful to you, tell them to stop in a calm, clear, respectful way. If this does not work, tell them again or find an adult you trust to help you work things out.

Remember that you can look for other people to be friends with. The world is full of wonderful people who can be fun, respectful, kind, and terrific friends – you just need to find them. And you won't be able to do this if you hang out with people who are not acting like good friends.

Know Your Choices

At age nine, my son Arend came home from school absolutely furious. "Today, that *awful* girl threw my shoe into the girl's bathroom and you *know* I can't go into the girl's bathroom," he stormed, clearly feeling outraged. "I had to walk in my socks in the hall until the yard duty teacher got my shoe back for me."

"That sounds embarrassing!" I said, managing not to laugh at his indignation. "Was there anything else?"

"*Yes*!" Arend exploded. "Every single day, when my best friend and I are building a construction out of sand in our spot in the school yard, that awful girl always comes and messes it up."

"How frustrating!" I exclaimed. Resisting the temptation to make suggestions, I asked, "What have you tried?"

"We've tried letting her help us, but it just doesn't work," Arend grumbled. "*That girl* takes over and breaks up our tunnel to make a castle. We've tried telling her to stop and leave us alone, but she just laughs at us. She pushes us out of the way and kicks our construction apart on purpose. We've tried telling the yard duty and everybody talks it out, but the same thing happens the next day."

Having safe friends is one of the best protections against bullying.

"*My goodness*!" I said sympathetically. "You've tried everything I know how to do. But I know a lot of people who are experts at protecting themselves. Do you want me to ask them?"

"Go ahead," my son replied gloomily. "But I think it won't do any good. This is hopeless."

I did ask my colleagues and shared their ideas with Arend the following week, starting with Timothy who helped me start Kidpower and who is a martial artist. "Timothy says that your project is like your personal space and at school you should have the right to defend it. He suggested that you stand in front of your construction and tell the girl to leave it alone. If she tries to come closer after being warned, keeping moving to stay between her and your structure. Start shouting, 'GO AWAY! LEAVE NOW! HELP!'

"Sooner or later, this girl will have to push or shove you to get you out of the way. If that happens, she has started the fight. You have my permission to do one bully technique like the shin kick and then go tell the teacher. You'll probably get in trouble with the school, but you won't get in trouble with me."

"What else?" Arend asked, very surprised and interested.

I then told him what Lisa, who is an expert in teaching women's self-defense, had thought. "Lisa says that this would be considered harassment if a boy were doing it to a girl. Harassment means bothering someone on purpose over and over. Lisa suggests that, if this girl is about to attack your project, you can put your arms together in front of you to make a wall. You can then walk towards her, so that you move her away without hitting her. As you do this, you can yell out what is happening so that everybody hears you."

"Go on," Arend said.

I smiled at my son and told him about Kimberly, who is a metaphysical therapist. "Kimberly says that you could imagine a very old, wise man with an extremely long white beard sitting high on top of a mountain who you could tell your troubles to and ask for help."

"You have some very interesting friends, Mom," Arend grinned.

I had saved the silliest for last, which was an idea from Mark, who builds the protective equipment for our head-to-toe padded instructors and whose business is called Nutcase Armor. "I don't recommend this, but Mark says that you could go into the bathroom and fill a toy water pistol with pee. Then, you could squirt that girl with it the next time she bothers you."

With his usual exuberance, Arend roared with laughter. He kept laughing until he toppled over, holding his sides and rolling across the floor.

I heard no more about the problem after that and asked a couple weeks later how things were going.

"Oh," Arend said nonchalantly. "Ever since you told me what your friends suggested, that girl has left us alone. I didn't have to say or do anything at all." Astonishing, I thought. Maybe something in Arend's attitude changed for this girl to stop so suddenly. Somehow just knowing that he had choices made things better.

Write Things Down

During a workshop for a youth group of twelve-year-old friends, my students wanted to know how to solve a problem with one girl in their class. "We're not supposed to leave anybody out at school, but she is so mean," they complained. "We'll be talking at lunch, and she'll interrupt to say something that hurts someone's feelings. When we tell her to stop, she says that we didn't understand her or that we are making it up."

We practiced some different speaking up tactics. The girls were doubtful about anything working, because their teacher was not willing to help. "Our teacher says that we just have to learn to get along," the girls explained. "We feel bad because we want to include this girl. We are used to having lots of different people as friends. But it's not fair to have to sit at lunch with somebody who is making putdown remarks. We can't ever just relax and have a nice conversation. Isn't there anything else we can do?"

"Well," I said. "This might not work either, but sometimes writing things down has an amazing amount of power. You could each bring little writing pads and keep them next to you at lunch. The minute this girl says something rude, pick up your journals and write it down.

"If the girl asks what you are doing, as is very likely, you can say that you are keeping track of the times she or anyone else makes putdown remarks and of exactly what she says. Tell her that, to be fair, you are also writing down what other people said before and after she made the remark. Explain that you want to document the problem because you want to have a lunchtime that is free of putdowns. Doing this might help this girl pay better attention to what she is saying and it might get your teacher to take your problem more seriously."

I didn't tell my students this, but writing things down would also make them more self-aware of their own behavior, in case that was a part of the problem.

Figuring out Different Solutions to Bullying Problems

1 Encourage young people to tell you what they have already tried. Act out the problem so that they can show you what they are doing, in case there are ways to increase their assertiveness. See the *Assertive Advocacy* section below to help define the difference between being passive, aggressive, and assertive.

2 Brainstorm to come up with new ideas. Sometimes making up silly plans to be able to laugh at a problem is extremely effective.

3 Help young people think of the differences between safe and unsafe friends. Even if someone is very fun, encourage them to be willing to let go of a friendship if it is not working. Realize that they might need time to grieve over a lost friendship, even if the former friend was very unkind.

4 Encourage young people to document problems by writing down what happened, what they tried, and what they want to see happen. This might solve the problem, and putting their thoughts into writing is excellent practice.

5 Remember that adults are responsible for ensuring that children and youth are in schools and activities that promote their emotional and physical safety. Remind children that, no matter how busy or tired you are, you want them to tell you when they have problems. Supervise what young people are doing, intervene if need be, and if nothing else works, consider the option of changing schools or youth activities.

Chapter Fifteen

Stopping Cyber-Bullying

Being Hurtful with Greater Efficiency and Anonymity
Ensuring Responsible Use of Technology
Documenting and Reporting Cyber-Bullying Problems
Create a Written Communication Technology Safety Contract
Actions Adults Can Take to Help Prevent and Stop Cyber-Bullying

Computers and mobile devices can add to our children's lives academically and socially. Technological literacy is an important skill set that they will need throughout their lives, and kids can benefit from opportunities to develop skill and confidence using all kinds of technology in age-appropriate ways.

Computers and mobile devices have also created new ways to cause harm. Cyber-bulling, for example, is just one new way to cause harm made possible by technology. Adult guidance and clear boundaries are necessary to support kids in learning to use technology in ways that are safe for everyone.

Being Hurtful with Greater Efficiency and Anonymity

When I first heard about cyber-bullying many years ago, no one had come up with a name for it yet, and it happened between adults. A friend of a friend had an anonymous e-mail about her sent out to hundreds of people at her work with false accusations and vivid, hurtful, personal remarks. A man I know who is a devout Jew had a message sent to thousands of people at his company from his e-mail address with horrific Jew-bashing remarks. In both cases, the impact was devastating.

The anonymous nature and speed of the Internet and text messages on cell phones have created new opportunities for bullying. Technology-savvy kids can easily:

• Use instant messaging or text messages to reach hundreds or even thousands of people with cruel language, mean jokes, information given in confidence, or rumors;

• Create Web pages or chat rooms to make direct threats and insults or to attack the reputation and credibility of others;

• Take photos of people with a cell phone or digital camera without their knowledge or permission, doctor the photos to make them more embarrassing, and disperse them widely;

• Log onto someone's account, post false information, change existing

With cyber-bullying, the ease of being anonymous and of reaching many people all at once can make the target feel a great sense of violation and helplessness.

Bullying is bullying – whether it is done with paper, words, actions or electrons.

information, and send out negative messages as if these came from that person; and

• Create upsetting listings about someone with insulting or threatening remarks or start rumors through on-line friend communities such as Myspace, Friendster, and Facebook.

Often young people play with technology because doing something just because they have the power to do it seems interesting. When they don't see the immediate result of their actions, they might not realize that what they are doing is destructive. Just as with other forms of bullying behavior, some kids do this to be funny, without thinking through the harm they might be doing to someone else. They tell themselves, "I was just joking." Or, "I was just texting." Others do it because they are angry or because being able to have this level of impact on someone else gives them a sense of power.

With cyber-bullying, the ease of being anonymous and of reaching many people all at once can make the target feel a great sense of violation and helplessness.

Many adults are far less familiar with new technology than their children and become overwhelmed by the many creative ways that technology can be used to hurt, scare, or embarrass people directly and through damaging their reputation.

We all need to recognize cyber-bullying for what it is – a modern version of the ancient problem of people being mean to each other. Bullying is bullying – whether it is done with paper, words, actions, or electrons.

Ensuring Responsible Use of Technology
Just as with other activities, adults need to know and supervise what young people are doing with technology. Remind young people that the "problems should not be secrets" rule applies to the use of technology. Be very clear that use of technology is a privilege, not a right.

The message we want young people to have is that, "Your job is to take responsibility for preventing any harm done by your actions. When you communicate something either by yourself or with others – whether it is by e-mail, Web site, user group, text messaging, telephone, fax, mail, notes, conversations, drawings, facial expressions, words, gestures, photos, signs, billboards, or pony express – you are responsible for the results. The same thing is true when you throw a stone – no matter what your intentions are, you are responsible for where it lands and what damage it does."

Keep the computers young people are using in a public space. Sit with children and teens so that you can see what they are doing. Even if you don't understand the technology, you have more life experience than your children do. Be their "co-pilot" with technology by having your kids show you what they are doing and how it works.

Stay up-to-date on what to watch out for. Your Internet provider can help you choose a system that will help you to monitor your children's on-line activity if you decide that this is a good idea. My personal recommendation is that adults be involved enough that this kind of monitoring is not necessary, but every family is different.

If you give your children wireless phones, make an informed decision about whether or not to allow them to use text messaging or to send and receive photos. Even if these features are included in the cell phone package, you can forbid or limit their use. These features can be fun and they can also be easily misused.

Together with your children, look up their names in on-line social networking communities and search engines to see what is listed about them. Legally, private information about people under eighteen requires parental permission to be made public, but there is no substitute for checking directly. Parents or guardians have the right to insist that their children do not put their names, photos, or other personal information anywhere on the Internet without prior permission.

Make sure that young people are aware that, if someone knows their password or has access to their e-mail, this person can send out messages from their e-mail address. If one person has their photo, countless people can have their photo. Anything they post on the Internet can become public information that a parent or future employer might see.

Teachers can build understanding by having students use the Internet to look up cyber-bullying examples and the harmful results. A school assignment could be to write an essay or make posters about what cyber-bullying is, why it is wrong, and how to stop it. Schools can have students sign pledges about not participating in any forms of bullying or harassment, including this one. Families can do the same.

Part of the solution is simply to give them information. We tell young people in our workshops that cyber-bullying is illegal. Police and other adults can usually figure out who sent the messages. Worried students often come up and ask, "It's *really* illegal? Can someone *really* tell?"

Documenting and Reporting Cyber-Bullying Problems

When people see an upsetting message on their computer or wireless phone, wanting to get rid of it or to answer it are both normal responses.

Instead, document the problem. Warn young people not to reply to any attacking messages, as tempting as it might be to try to defend their reputation by answering, and not to delete cyber-bullying messages, even if they are embarrassing.

Tell young people to save upsetting messages and to let you know when they think they are being cyber-bullied. Make copies of the messages to document what happened. Ask your cell phone company or your Internet provider for help on tracking down the source. Ask what their policy is and insist that they take action. Sometimes, the first person you go to in a company is not that helpful, so be prepared to insist on going up the chain

Clear rules and guidelines can help to prevent computer safety problems.

of command until you find someone who has the authority and the skills to address the problem.

If your child is having a problem and classmates are the most likely culprits, go to the school principal and classroom teacher to report what happened. Show them the messages and ask what action they are going to take to protect your child. If they don't show concern, say, "My child's privacy and safety have been violated. We need your help." Find out what the school policy is about stopping all forms of bullying, including cyber-bullying.

If the messages include any kind of threat, report the problem to the police.

Create a Written Communication Technology Safety Contract
Written contracts are useful in defining expectations and in learning about taking agreements seriously. Adapt the following contract, which is available for downloading on our website, for your child. Discuss or modify each point to make sure you have a clear, workable agreement. Then, have your child initial each item as well as signing the contract. Update and make a new contract at least once a year.

Contract Defining Terms of Youth Access to Communication Technology

I, [name of child] _____
understand that my use of communication technology such as wireless phones, mobile digital devices, telephones, postal services, any social networking sites, computers, telegrams, or the pony express is a privilege, not a right. I understand that my adults incur monetary costs and also assume significant financial and legal risks when they allow me to use these tools for communication. I understand that "my adults" refers to my parent(s) or legal guardian(s).

I agree to be safe and respectful in my use of any of these communication tools, whether they are my own or belong to someone else. I agree to make the following commitments in exchange for the privilege of using any communication technology, and I understand that any level of access to communication technology relies upon my upholding these agreements:

1. I will get permission from my adults each time before I give out any personal information through the Internet, wireless communication devices, or to people I don't already know well. Personal information means anything that could identify me or my family, including any of our full names, addresses, home/cell /work phone numbers, photographs, details about where any of us live or go to school or participate in recreational activities, etc. _____ (Initial)

2. I will do my best to stay in places on the Internet or in the real world that I've agreed on with my adults – places that are interesting, safe, and fun, but not inappropriate or scary. If anything I come across makes me uncomfortable or is inappropriate, I will tell my parents. _____ (Initial)

3. I will Check First with my adult before I change our plan about where I am going, what I am doing, and whom I am with - whether we are together virtually (through technology) or physically (in the real world). I will never

agree to meet with anyone I've met online without getting permission from my adults FIRST. Even if permission is granted, I will meet someone I've met online only in a pubic place accompanied by an adult my adults approve of. _____ (Initial)

4. I will not send anything to anyone in any form that I do not want the whole world to read or see. I will Check First with my adults to get permission before sending or posting my picture or anything else that could possible identify me, my family, or other people I know. _____ (Initial)

5. I understand that files can be sent through the Internet that are potentially dangerous to our computers or to people emotionally. I will Check First with my parent(s), legal guardian(s), and teachers before I download anything from the Internet or click on a link that is unknown, even if it looks sort of familiar. _____ (Initial)

6. I will not be mean to others through communication technology or in other ways, even as a joke. I will not pass on unkind information or rumors about other people – kids or adults – except to give it to my adults to have it reported. I will not say I "Like" something that is negative about someone else. I will not pass on someone's photos or messages without that person's permission as well as the permission of my adults. _____ (Initial)

7. I understand that others might try to bully me through technology or in other ways – and that, if this happens, it is not my fault. If anything makes me uncomfortable or upset, I agree that I will not respond to the person bullying; I will save the messages and print them if I can; and I will get help from my adults to report the problem and to make sure that I get support so that I do not feel alone. _____ (Initial)

8. I understand that spending too much time using technology can become unsafe and/or unhealthy, especially if my technology use interferes with sleeping, being outside, studying, reading, exercising, or doing things with people. I agree to follow my family and school rules about when and how long I can be online or sending and reading messages of any kind. _____ (Initial)

9. If I think that any part of this agreement does not work and needs to be changed, I will still fully uphold the agreement. I will discuss what needs to be changed with my adults and get their agreement to the change ahead of time rather than breaking their rules. _____ (Initial)

10. I understand that nobody is perfect and that mistakes are part of learning. If I make a mistake and don't follow any of these agreements, I will tell my adults rather trying to hide it or feeling bad about it. _____ (Initial)

I understand that this is an important contract and I agree to do my best to meet all of these agreements. I understand that the consequences for failing to uphold any part of this agreement may include:

• complete loss of access to communication technology for the amount of

time determined by my adults;
- significant restrictions on my use of technology, even if I am allowed to keep it in my possession;
- additional consequences intended to address any physical or emotional injury, financial loss, or other damage resulting from my misuse of communication technology.

Signature of Child/Teen: _____

Signature of Parent/Guardian: _____

Signature of Parent/Guardian: _____

Date:____

We agree to revisit this contract in one year but agree that this contract will remain valid until a replacement contract is agreed upon and signed by all parties involved.

Actions Adults Can Take to Help Prevent and Stop Cyber-Bullying

1   *Co-Pilot With Your Child.* **Many kids have more technological knowledge than their parents, but parents still have more life experience about what is safe and what is not safe. Whether your technical knowledge is a little or a lot, sit with your children and have them show you how they use the Internet and their cell phones. Co-piloting means that you go together so that you can understand how your child is using technology, stay aware of what your child is doing, and agree on safety rules.**

2   *Keep technology use public rather than private.* **Whether your children are texting on a cell phone, doing social networking even through school-approved activities, exploring the Internet, or using e-mail, stay aware of what they are doing, whom they are doing it with, and where they are going. Know how often and how long your child is spending using technology rather than doing other things such as sleeping, being with people, reading, exercising, etc.**

3   *Discuss the issue.* **Ask children and youth what they already know about cyber-bullying. You might be amazed at how much they can tell you. Ask if this has ever happened to them or anyone they know. Make sure that the young people in your life know that:**
- **Cyber-bullying means using computers, wireless phones, social networks, and other technology to hurt, scare, or embarrass other people. It is illegal and unethical.**
- **Being mean is being mean, no matter how you do it. Don't ask if it's funny. Ask if it will make someone unhappy.**
- **Even if you think someone was mean to you, being mean back is not a safe way to handle the problem. Instead, get help from an adult you trust.**
- **Have the courage to *speak up* if you notice anyone cyber-bullying. Say that this is wrong and that you are *not* going to keep it a secret.**
- **Never post anything on the Internet or send something electronically that you don't want the world to see.**
- **If you get an upsetting message or see something that is attacking you: *Do not reply. Do not delete. Save* the message, print it if you can and *get help* from an adult you trust. If one adult does not help you, keep asking until you get the help you need.**

4   *Be clear about the rules.* **The use of computers for anything except schoolwork is a privilege. The use of wireless phones for anything except for emergencies and communication with parents is also a privilege. These privileges will be lost if they are used for unsafe or hurtful purposes. You expect your children to stay in charge of what they say and do, to tell you about problems, and to get your agreement in advance about any changes. Use the *Communication Technology Safety Contract* discussed above and available on the Kidpower website or create your own.**

(Continued on next page.)

5 *Stay involved.* Spend time with young people so that you know what they are doing. Do things that are fun together that do not involve the use of technology.

6 *Be careful.* Unless this is within a secure system of people who know each other, such as a school, do not allow your children to post personal information or photos in an on-line social network or website.

7 *Give consequences.* If your child bullies, whether through technology or by some other means, have the child apologize and make amends. Give an appropriate related consequence, depending on what happened. Be prepared to pull the plug on all uses of technology for a specific period of time, so that the concept that this use is a privilege, not a right, is reinforced.

8 *Provide help.* If your child is hurt by cyber-bullying, give the child emotional support by saying, "I am so sorry this is happening to you and so proud of you for having the courage to tell me. This is not your fault, and we are going to do what we can to make it stop." Ask for help from school authorities, your Internet provider or cell phone company, and, if necessary, the police.

9 *Practice.* Use ideas from the *Being Brave* chapter to define what cyber-bullying might look like, how to speak up, what a negative reaction might be, and what an effective response could be. Let children make up their own story to use for the practice. Switch roles with them.

For example, a friend might say, "I can't stand Roger. Look, I got a photo of him going to the bathroom on the field trip. Let's see how many people we can send this to."

One way to speak up could be: "That's cyber-bullying. It's wrong."

A common negative reaction to this boundary is, "But you have to admit that it would be funny."

An effective response might be, "Even though Roger is not my favorite person, I don't think it is funny to embarrass people. Besides, it is illegal."

Chapter Sixteen

Practice as a Management Tool For Unsafe, Disrespectful Behavior

Ask, "How could you have done this more safely?" Then, practice the safer solution.

"Let's practice making safer choices!"
Remember that Children Often Want to Do Something that Their Adults Think is a Bad Idea
Set a Good Example by Accepting and Managing Your Upset Feelings
Lecturing or Arguing Don't Help
Address Resistance with Creativity, Compassion, and Humor
Find Opportunities to Turn Problems into Practices
Practicing Solutions to Different Kinds of Problems

When children say or do things that are hurtful, rude, destructive, or potentially dangerous, parents and teachers can find themselves trying to manage this behavior by explaining, scolding, discussing, and using rewards and punishments. Too often, these strategies make life unpleasant without solving the problem.

Practicing Kidpower skills can be a highly effective management tool for addressing emotionally or physically unsafe behavior. Kidpower's Positive Practice Method puts the focus on what you want the children to do in order to prevent a problem like this from happening again. Using this approach as a management tool does not take long; does not require that you believe one party or the other; and is productive rather than punitive.

"Let's practice making safer choices!"
Recently, a kindergarten teacher told me how she had used the Positive Practice Method in her classroom after a little boy had kicked another in the crotch. The boys were resistant, but the teacher said, "Instead of making the same mistakes, let's practice making safer choices!

The teacher coached both boys to imagine they were being bothered and to make a fence with their hands, while saying in a loud voice, "STOP! I DON'T LIKE THIS!" She then had both boys practice using their Walk Away Power to leave. They also practiced their Hands Down Power by first imagining that they felt like touching someone or something that they shouldn't or felt like hitting, and then by using their power to pull their arms to their sides and keep them there.

This teacher reported that, later, she noticed the boy who had gotten kicked begin to bother the boy who had kicked him. This time, instead of kicking, he made his fence and set his boundary. The other little boy, who had meant no harm, immediately stopped!

This teacher's story inspired a skill that we now call "Feet Down Power" as a technique to help a child remember NOT to kick. To practice Feet Down Power, imagine that you really feel like kicking someone. Instead of kicking, pretend that your feet are glued to the ground and use your power to keep them there or to move them only enough that you can walk away.

Here are some Kidpower guidelines for how to use the Positive Practice Method as an effective, respectful behavior management tool with children.

Remember that Children Often Want to Do Something That Their Adults Think is a Bad Idea

Young people don't know. They forget. They experiment with testing boundaries or with negative uses of their power. Our rules are not nearly as important to children as our rules are to us. Instead of seeing "bad" behavior as a failure for ourselves or our children, we can use these problems as opportunities for children to learn. The point of having them practice skills is not to punish them but to give them chances to show how they can use their skills to handle real-life situations.

Set a Good Example by Accepting and Managing Your Upset Feelings

Whether your toddler just climbed high up a ladder or your teenager swore at her mother, getting upset about emotionally destructive or physically dangerous behavior is completely normal. Rather than trying to suppress your feelings of annoyance, sadness, shock, worry, frustration, or anger when your child does something upsetting, accept your right to have these feelings. And then, in order to deal with the problem safely and effectively, manage your feelings instead of letting them cause you to shut down, get frantic, or explode.

You can practice for yourself by imagining your child doing something dangerous or destructive and then getting centered. Take a deep breath. Feel where your hands and feet are. Straighten your back. Look at or imagine seeing something calming. Remember that you can choose to look at the problem behavior as a chance for everyone to strengthen relationships and learn important life skills.

Lecturing or Arguing Don't Help

Suppose that two kids are fighting and you didn't see it start. Avoid playing the judge and deciding whose story to believe. Instead, you can point out that they were both doing something unsafe – fighting – and that you want to see each of them practice how to make safe choices. Then, coach them to practice skills such as: using their awareness to notice that someone is getting upset; saying, "Please stop"; stopping when someone sets a reasonable boundary; walking away; using Hands Down Power and Mouth Closed Power; and getting help.

Instead of seeing "bad" behavior as a failure for ourselves or our children, we can use these problems as opportunities for children to learn.

Address Resistance with Creativity, Compassion, and Humor

How many of us really *like* being told that you've done something wrong? Most of us hate it, and most kids feel the same way. Resistance can include:

• Saying, "I don't want to!" and protesting bitterly
• Rolling eyes and sighing heavily
• Making rude remarks and sarcastic jokes
• Arguing or minimizing with comments like, "I said I'm sorry so why are you punishing me?" Or, "I already know, and this is a big waste of time!"

Rather than taking a young person's resistance personally or getting stuck trying to talk her or him into agreeing with you, you can calmly persist with compassion, creativity, and humor. You can communicate a message along the lines of, "I understand. However, no matter how this problem started, I felt that what happened was unsafe (unkind, against our values, etc.). I appreciate what you are saying, but you are more likely to remember if we practice."

Your goal is to make practicing interesting and even fun, rather than to "punish" the child. For a younger child, you could start with a demonstration with puppets or toys to show the problem behavior and then to show safer choices. You could let older children or teens "practice" using spice jars or other unlikely objects as characters to act out the problems themselves and to show different safe and unsafe options. You might act out the practice yourself first; then, have your child take a turn.

Find Opportunities to Turn Problems into Practices

People tell us they are using practice to address many kinds of unsafe behavior. For example, a parent with a toddler who was always running off told her child before going to the store, "It is not safe for you to leave my side when we go to the park or the store. Let's practice staying together. If you don't want me to hold on to you, then you need to show me how you can hold on to me." They practiced, and, with some reminding, her toddler held onto her.

Parents worried about their teens driving with friends have had them practice speaking up about too fast or distracted driving to show that they can as a requirement of getting permission to go.

Sometimes, people worry that the language we teach children to use does not sound like what "real children" or "real teens" would normally say. As adults, our job is to young people how to behave in ways that often *don't* come naturally to them so that they can stay safe, have positive relationships, and get the most out of their lives. We encourage children and teens to try using our language and then to find words that work for them as long as these are both clear and respectful.

Practicing Solutions to Different Kinds of Problems

Problem: A preschooler is grabbing a toy from another child, who is shoving her away.
Practice 1: Each child says, "I'm using this now. You can have it when I'm done."
Practice 2: Each child reaches out to shove and then uses Hands Down Power to stop.
Practice 3: Each child says, "I've waited a long time. I'd like a turn."
Practice 4: Each child takes turns letting go of the toy. Each child goes to look for another toy.

Problem: Two children are roughhousing in a way that was fun at first but then got overwhelming for one of them. One is crying, and the other is calling him a "crybaby".
Practice 1: Each child says, "Stop that game! I don't feel comfortable. Let's play something else."
Practice 2: Each child pretends to want to keep roughhousing, but uses Hands Down Power, Feet Down Power, and Mouth Closed Power.
Practice 3: Each child uses the Trash Can to throw away the word "crybaby". Each child practices saying out loud, "My feelings are important."

Problem: Two teens are shouting insults at each other.
Practice 1: Each shows ways to "dispose of" insults without attacking the other person instead of taking the insults inside.
Practice 2: Each pretends to feel upset and demonstrates Getting Centered and Using Walk Away Power with a calm, aware, and confident attitude.
Practice 3: Each demonstrates Feeling One Way and Acting Another.

Sometimes, more complex social dynamics have developed that require separating the children for different kinds of practices. Suppose one child is constantly being left out of games, conversations, and other activities by the other children. Unfortunately, this child whines a lot, wants to get her way all the time, and makes putdown remarks about other children, which is why they say it's not fun to play with her.

Practices for the child being left out: Speaking in a regular voice rather than whining. Using Mouth Closed Power instead of making putdown remarks. Waiting your turn. Asking in a cheerful voice, "Excuse me. Can I play." Apologizing and persisting in the face of rejection by saying with a cheerful, assertive attitude, "I know I've sometimes been impatient and rude. I'm sorry. I'm working on changing. I'd really like to play!" Getting help using a regular voice and being specific about what happened without being attacking or insulting.

Practices for the other children in being inclusive while taking care of themselves: Giving people another chance even when you don't feel like it by saying 'yes' together with a boundary, such as, "Yes, but no hitting." Stopping people without attacking them when they say or do something that is rude. Saying, "That was a rude thing to say. Please stop!" Saying, "Excuse me! It's MY turn now." Saying, "Please use a regular voice." When things get stuck, getting help using a regular voice, and being specific about what happened without being attacking or insulting.

In addition to addressing behavior problems, the Positive Practice Method can be helpful for many other potential challenges: meeting new people when you go to a new place; recovering from a mistake when you are playing a sport without feeling bad about yourself or blaming someone else; asking someone to dance at a party; preparing for an important interview; etc. The steps are:
• Define the problem or challenge in objective terms, without judging anyone's character or intent
• Identify, very specifically and realistically, what you want to see happen
• Rehearse the behavior necessary to make the outcome you want possible, with coaching in how to do this effectively

Chapter Seventeen

Common Questions About Bullying

Practicing safety skills can be fun

1. How Will I Know if My Child Is Being Bullied?
2. What Should I Do if My Child Is Being Bullied at School?
3. What if My Child Is Bullying Other Kids?
4. Should I Say Anything to the Parents of a Child Who Is Bullying Mine?
5. What if a Teacher Is Doing the Bullying?
6. How Can I Teach Kids to Tell the Difference Between Someone Acting Friendly or Being a True Friend?

In the Kidpower office, we receive e-mails and calls from parents, teachers, and other caring adults from all over the world who are looking for answers for how to address bullying. Many decisions become easier when everyone decides to Put Safety First - ahead of worries about embarrassing, bothering, or upsetting others. We want to find solutions that take into account the overwhelming and conflicting demands faced by schools, youth groups, and other places that have responsibility for the safety of the young people in their care. Here are some of the most commonly asked questions.

How Will I Know if My Child Is Being Bullied?
Sometimes children will tell their adults right away if they have a problem with being bullied. Sometimes they will suffer in silence until they suddenly break down. Make sure that you tell children repeatedly that you want to know when they have problems, and make sure you listen compassionately to their answers.

Symptoms of being bullied might include:
• Having trouble sleeping;
• Having upset stomachs on school mornings;
• Being fearful about going to school or other youth activities;
• Coming home from school acting sad, gloomy, irritable, or unhappy;
• Coming home from school with unexplained bruises, cuts, and scratches;
• Being worried, anxious, or depressed;
• Saying mean things about her or himself; and/or
• Coming home with torn or damaged clothing, books, or other possessions.

What Should I Do if My Child Is Being Bullied at School?
We hear countless stories from upset parents whose children have been victimized at school.

"My thirteen-year-old son is a good kid who has never been in trouble. Sports are really important to him. A group of boys are always taunting him after games. Recently, he tried to argue with them instead of walking away. After these boys hit

him a couple of times, he hit back. Now he is kicked off his team. When I tried to talk with the school administrators, they believed the other boys and not him."

"My eleven-year-old daughter was teased because she has a disability. The teacher stopped the bullying, but never told my daughter that this was not her fault and never informed her father or me. Our daughter came home confused and worried, thinking that she was in trouble for causing a controversy."

"My twelve-year-old son endured months of another boy making up stories that were supposedly just for fun but that used his name as the anti-hero who was getting blown up or falling into pits or having things fall on him. The intention was clearly to humiliate my son. By the time he finally told me what was happening, he was failing his classes."

"My daughter goes to the first grade and likes to wear dresses. A couple of boys in her class started a game they called humping, where they sandwiched my little girl between them, pulling up her dress, trapping her and acting as if they were having sex with her. When I complained to the school, they talked with the boys, who are now calling my daughter names like 'stupid baby' and 'tattletale.'"

"When my daughter reported that she saw a gun at school, the boy who had the gun was expelled. But this boy's friends have started threatening my daughter in subtle ways that are hard to address. They make gestures like pointing their fingers as if they are shooting at her. They try to walk a little too close to her, almost knocking her down."

"My twelve-year-old son is young emotionally but looks older physically. Girls in his class are constantly making sexual remarks about his body, his clothes and what he says. He comes home feeling embarrassed and is starting to hate going to school."

School is a big part of children's lives. Because decisions about how and where children get an education are the responsibility of adults, the children themselves have no choice about being there. As caring adults, we expect schools to provide an environment that is emotionally and physically safe for our children.

Here are the steps to take when your child tells you about a problem at school:

1. Stay Calm.
As parents, feeling terrified and enraged about any kind of threat to the well-being of your children is normal. You probably want to fix the problem immediately and maybe to punish the people who caused your children to be hurt, embarrassed, or scared.

Instead of acting upset, your job is to act calm. If your child tells you about a problem, take a big breath and say in a calm, matter-of-fact voice, "I am so glad you are telling me this. I am sorry that this happened to you. Please tell me more about exactly what happened so we can figure out what to do. You deserve to feel safe and comfortable at school."

If your child did not tell you but you found out some other way, say calmly, "I saw this happen/heard about this happening. It looked/sounded like it might be unpleasant for you. Can you tell me more about it?"

Remember, if you act upset, your child is likely to get upset, too. She or he might want to protect you and her/himself from your reaction by not telling you about problems in the future or by denying that anything is wrong. The older a child is, the more important it is that the child is able to feel some control about any follow-up actions you might take with the school.

In addition, if you act upset when you are approaching school officials or the parents of children who are bothering your child, they are likely to become defensive. Nowadays, school administrators are often fearful of lawsuits, both from the parents of the child who was victimized and from the parents of the child who was accused of causing the problem. This is a real fear because a lawsuit can seriously drain the already limited resources of their school.

At the same time, most school administrators are deeply committed and truly want to address problems that affect the well-being of their students. They are far more likely to respond positively to parents who are approaching them in an objective and respectful way.

Please remember that teachers and school administrators are doing an incredibly difficult job. They are responsible for a large community of students and are often understaffed and have limited resources. Students come to them from many different backgrounds and life situations.

Teachers do not get to decide which students they will have in their classrooms and are often dealing with children and families with emotional and physical problems. In my experience, most teachers and administrators are good people who are trying to keep their students as safe, happy, and healthy as possible. Feeling very upset, anxious, and angry when you are worried about your child's well-being is normal, but remember that the professional educators who are responsible for your child during the day are usually caring individuals who deserve to be treated in a respectful way.

No matter how good a job you do, some people will react badly when they are first told about a problem. Don't let that stop you. Stay focused on your purpose, which is to explain what happened and what you want to see changed.

2. Get the whole story.
Avoid jumping to conclusions or making assumptions. Ask questions of your child in a calm, reassuring way. Ask questions of other people who might be involved, making it clear that your goal is to understand and figure out how to address the problem rather than to get even with anybody.

3. Look for solutions, not for blame.
Once you understand the situation, your goal is to find ways to repair any harm that was done and to prevent future problems. Try to assume that teachers and school administrators are overwhelmed and doing their best. They deserve support and acknowledgement for what they are doing right as well as to be told in a respectful way what is wrong.

Feeling very upset, anxious, and angry when you are worried about your child's well-being is normal, but remember that the professional educators are usually caring individuals who deserve to be treated in a respectful way.

Try to look at the issue from all perspectives. Is the problem caused because the school needs more resources in order to supervise children properly during recess and lunch or before and after school? Does the school need help formulating a clear policy that makes behavior that threatens, hurts, scares, or embarrasses others against the rules? Does your child need more practice to develop stronger personal safety skills? Does the child who harmed your child need help, too?

4. Make a plan to prevent future problems.
If the school doesn't have a clear plan in place for handling incidents, help them develop one. A plan should include:

• Stopping the behavior by a direct intervention and by making it clear that this behavior is against school rules;

• Protecting the child who was being bullied from further bullying or retaliation;
• Giving appropriate consequences to the children who did the bullying, depending on the nature of the bullying and the age of the children involved. If nothing else works, children who cannot stop themselves from being hurtful towards others need to be sent to the principal's office. The principal can involve parents and possibly other resource people in making a plan with the child to change this behavior;

• Giving reassurance to the child who was bullied that what happened was not her or his fault, even though people got in trouble for it;

• If the teacher's perception is that both parties are contributing to the problem, have both parties use a conflict resolution process to work things out and do role-playing of how to use personal safety skills to handle the problem differently in the future;

• Notifying the parents of all parties that the incident occurred and what was done about it; and

• Making the training and availability of resources for their staff, parents, and students a priority.

Children deserve to be in an environment that is emotionally and physically safe. Concerned parents can help schools find, fund, and implement age-appropriate programs that make a sustained, school-wide commitment to creating a culture of safety, respect, and caring rather than of competition, harassment, and disregard.

5. Protect your child for the long run.
Try to keep the big picture in mind as well as the immediate problem. What protecting your child means will vary depending on the ability of the school to resolve the problem, the nature of the problem, and on your child's needs.

Children can learn to walk away from people who are bothering them, to protect themselves emotionally and physically, and to ask for help sooner rather than later. Make practicing these skills a priority and consider training such as the kind offered by Kidpower. In some cases, protecting

Children deserve to be in an environment that is emotionally and physically safe.

your child might mean that you work together with the teacher, the school administrator, the parents of the other child, and all children involved to create a realistic plan to stop the problem. In other cases, the best solution for your child might be to change schools.

6. Get emotional support.
Don't ignore the feelings that come up, even if the problem is solved. Give support in the moment to the child, get support for yourself, and pay attention to whether these feelings persist. A few studies have indicated that some people have post-traumatic stress syndrome because of bullying. Sometimes the harassing and bullying of your child can bring up feelings from bad experiences out of your own past.

Parents often have to deal with guilt for not preventing the problem and sometimes struggle with rage. Getting support might mean talking issues over with other caring adults who can listen to you and your child with perspective and compassion. Getting support might mean going to a therapist or talking with counselors provided by the school or by other agencies.

7. Be realistic.
As parents, most of us want to protect our children from all harm. However, if we monitor their lives so closely that they never fall, never fail, and never get hurt or sad, then we would be depriving our children of having the room to grow. Upsetting experiences do not have to lead to long-term damage if children are listened to respectfully, if the problem is resolved, and if their feelings are supported. Young people can take charge of their safety by learning skills for preventing and stopping harassment themselves by setting boundaries, avoiding people whose behavior is problematic, and getting help when they need it.

What if My Child Is Bullying Other Kids?
Most parents want their children to be respectful to others, and they worry when they are not. Three typical worries are:

• "Sometimes my son calls other kids names and pushes them around to get what he wants."

• "My daughter encourages her friends to leave another girl out. They even tried making up stories to get her into trouble."

• "My kids are angels at school and mean to each other at home."

Here are some ways that parents can help stop their children from bullying others.

1. Have a strong, affectionate, and mutually respectful relationship with your children.
There is nothing more important in your life than your children. Have fun together. Give them the gift of your time. It's the only gift that will count in the long run. Model being a positive, powerful leader. Make it clear that you are in charge, but involve children in decision-making when you can. Accept their right to have all their feelings, even though they have to learn to

Give your children the gift of your time.

With help, children can usually learn how to identify a negative pattern, notice when it starts to happen, and find ways to change their behavior.

manage their behavior. Do the best you can to model the behavior you want them to have and acknowledge when you make mistakes.

Get help from parenting resources if you aren't sure what to do or feel stuck. These two very useful books written by Adele Faber and Elaine Mazlish are classics for parents: *How to Talk so Kids Will Listen* and *Listen so Kids Will Talk* and *Siblings Without Rivalry*.

2. Make the rules clear.
Show children that bullying behavior is not okay with you at home, at school, or anywhere you go. You want to know about it, and you want to find ways to stop it. Even if other people let their children behave that way, it is not okay with you for your children to behave that way. Even if other important adults in their lives behave that way, this is not the example you want your child to copy. Especially until children can tell you what happens when they are away from you, make sure that the people supervising your children have the same standards that you do.

3. Be realistic.
Bullying behavior in a child or teen rarely means that this young person has a permanent character flaw. Remember that grabbing what you want, ganging up on other people, being mean to be funny, and getting back at someone for perceived wrongs is normal behavior and is modeled for children all the time. The solution is to help young people to develop better social skills, more empathy, and better impulse control. Until they are able to manage themselves, young people need adult supervision.

4. Pay attention.
Stop bullying behavior sooner rather than later. If you want to give children the chance to handle the problem themselves, monitor the situation and step in to help them to be successful. Reminders of rules and coaching in the moment are far more effective than letting children flounder on their own.

5. Try to figure out why.
The purpose of knowing why is neither to blame nor to excuse, but to help you find effective solutions. Is this child still very young and learning? Did she forget? Was he not clear about the rules? Did she lose her temper? Does he lack problem-solving skills? Does she need to learn how to stop herself? Does he need to learn how to see the other person's point of view? Is the child copying someone else?

6. Have clear consequences.
Consequences should be framed as logical outcomes for the behavior rather than as punishments. For example:

• Apologizing;

• Making amends by doing a chore for the person who was bullied;

• Writing a letter or drawing a picture to show understanding of why this behavior is a problem;

- Role-playing what happened and practicing how to behave differently in the future;

- Sitting down for a few minutes to think things over instead of playing;

- Coming inside to be with the adult and away from other kids for a little while; and

- Losing some privilege like watching television or playing on the computer for a specific time period.

Do your best *not* to be angry when you give consequences. Be thoughtful. Avoid repeated threats of consequences that the child will see as negative. Instead, give one warning or reminder and then follow through. You want children to see you as having the integrity of meaning what you say and the fairness of having the consequence fit the behavior. If both children created the problem, both children should have the consequences

Sometimes bullying grows out of a dynamic between two children. They might have developed patterns of bothering each other that lead to problems. With help, children can usually learn how to identify a negative pattern, notice when it starts to happen, and find ways to change their behavior.

7. Be prepared for children to resist.
Children might deny what happened even if you saw everything – not because they are deliberately lying, but because they don't want to feel like they are bad, and selective memory screens things out. Children might say, "I don't care!" – not because they don't care, but because they don't want to feel bad. They might say, "I hate you!" – not because they don't love you, but because they hate having you tell them what to do. They might blame the other person – not because they really believe this, but because they don't want to have to blame themselves. Children might need you to set their boundaries for them because they have not yet learned to set boundaries within themselves.

When children resist, parents can acknowledge their feelings and re-state the expectation. Sometimes children need a little time to themselves to cool off before they are ready to listen.

8. Help children develop "People Safety" and other social-emotional skills.
Give children the chance to practice some of the personal safety skills described in this book in order to stop themselves from bullying. For example, you might have a child practice throwing a mean word in the trash can instead of getting caught up in name-calling. You might have a child practice walking away and getting help instead of getting into a fight. As they become old enough to understand, you can teach children about different kinds of bullying and why this is wrong.

Younger children need to learn how to ask for what they want instead of grabbing. People of all ages need to learn how to negotiate win-win solutions. Disappointments are part of life, and learning how to handle them without being destructive includes learning how to calm down and think

Help children negotiate win-win solutions.

first when you are upset, learning to wait your turn, and finding other things to do when you cannot get what you want.

Learning to understand other points of view is a major life skill. Most young people can develop empathy for others by hearing stories, by learning about feelings, and by being treated with empathy themselves.

Should I Say Anything to the Parents of a Child Who Is Bullying Mine?

The right answer to this question depends on the individuals involved and how important this relationship is to you or to your child.

Some parents definitely want to know and will be very thankful. Others might get upset and start blaming their child, your child, or you. What kind of a relationship do you have? What do you know about this person? Is this something that you are best off doing with the help of a neutral person such as the principal or teacher? Do you think that this parent already knows or not?

When possible, find ways to take charge of the environment your child is in. You can work with your child's youth group, sports team, dance club, or school to ensure that there is a written policy about bullying and educate everyone about what it means, including parents and kids.

Keep an eye out on how things are going and step in when you see a problem. Rather than seeing this as disciplining another person's child, take the position that you are ensuring safe behavior of all the children according to the policies the adults have agreed on. Instead of asking children why they have done something hurtful, just set a specific boundary, such as, "Please stop. Leaving people out/saying mean things/pushing is against the rules here."

If you decide to approach the parent, start with appreciation. For example, you might say something like, "I appreciate all you do for our kids and think your daughter is a lovely girl and a natural leader. However, I worry that she is experimenting with negative uses of her power in a way that is often hurtful to my daughter. Sometimes she (leaves people out/etc.). I'd like your help to make a plan where we can intervene when that happens in a way that is supportive to everyone.

Try to avoid labels like "bullying" and stay with the specific facts. For example, "I have something to tell you that is uncomfortable. I am doing this because I would want someone to tell me if the situation were reversed. My daughter says that she doesn't want to come to your house anymore because your son keeps hurting her. Games that start out fun often get too rough, and your son has a hard time listening when my daughter tells him to stop. Also, your son tries to stop my daughter from playing with other kids."

Parents who don't know what to do often minimize their child's bullying behavior. No matter how carefully and kindly you express your concern, don't be surprised is this parent says something attacking about you or your child. Practice what you are going to say out loud ahead of time. Be prepared for negative reactions so you can persist in stating your concern in a positive way.

Don't try to argue. Just say, "Thank you for telling me." This parent might get upset. Stay calm and say something like, "I don't mean to upset you. Again, I am putting myself in your shoes and doing what I would want you to do for me. It is normal for children to have trouble with boundaries sometimes."

Be prepared to offer support. Listen compassionately if this parent expresses frustration or despair in how to help her or his child. Mention books, parenting classes, and other resources that have been helpful to you.

Help children to identify when someone is acting like a "true friend."

What if A Teacher Is Doing the Bullying?
Most teachers are extremely caring individuals, but a few misuse their power. They might be sarcastic, demeaning, or otherwise act in ways that tear down the self-esteem of a child. Parents need to monitor potential problems with adults in the same way that they monitor other types of bullying behavior.

Take the time to observe what is actually happening in your child's classroom and on the schoolyard. Listen when your child complains about the teacher "being mean" and brainstorm solutions. Often, all a child needs is a sympathetic ear.

If you do think that your child's teacher is acting in a bullying way, don't let it go. It is poor modeling to excuse rude behavior by saying, "That's just the way she or he is." Instead, insist that the professionals caring for your children keep their temper, express their own boundaries firmly and politely, and set a good example of respectful, powerful adult leadership.

If you think that your child's teacher's behavior is a problem, remember that acting upset can be counter-productive. Reach out to your child's teacher with your concerns as described above in the question: *What if My Child Is Being Bullied at School?* Use any problems as an opportunity to model speaking up and being clear about boundaries.

How Can I Teach Kids to Tell the Difference Between Someone Acting Friendly or Being a True Friend?
We hear many sad stories about young people who were confused by others who pretended to be friendly in order to get their way, but whose actual intent was to get something from them or even to cause them harm. Here are typical examples:

One kindergarten teacher said, *"A few of my students are so charismatic that all the other kids want to be friends with them. Sometimes they will try to control other children by saying that they will only be their friend if they agree not to play with anyone else. I tell my students that real friends don't try to stop you from having other friends."*

One mother said, *"My seven-year-old daughter got into big trouble because a girl she really liked trashed the school bathroom by throwing paper towels into the toilets and sinks. This girl said that, since my daughter was her friend, my daughter had to blame another one of their classmates for making this mess."*

One father said, *"My ten-year-old son keeps getting tricked into doing another kid's homework because he wants so much to be accepted by him."*

People who deliberately use the trappings of friendship to get you to lower your boundaries... can break your heart

One middle school boy said, *"Some girls in our school go along with sex because they want to be popular. I feel bad because some guys tell these girls how much they care about them and then make horrible jokes about what sluts they are behind their backs."*

One teacher of a developmentally delayed teen said, *"Kids in his neighborhood pretended to be his friends and then persuaded him to steal my cell phone because they told him they needed the money."*

No matter how old or young you are, people who deliberately use the trappings of friendship to get you to lower your boundaries and do what they want can break your heart.

Both children and adults need to know that someone who smiles at you, says kind things to you, does nice things for you, and seems funny might be enjoyable to be with, but that this friendly behavior by itself does not make this person a trustworthy friend.

At the same time, having misunderstandings and crossing boundaries are normal communication problems in important relationships. Also, sometimes people change, and friendships that worked for a while stop working.

The reality is that some mistakes are probably unavoidable. You have to be willing to take some risks in order to get to know someone well enough to decide whether or not to keep this person as a friend.

So, how do you tell the difference between someone who is behaving in a way that is likable and someone who is going to be a good bet as a friend?

You have to judge by what a person does not just part of the time, but all of the time, and not just with you, but with everyone, in order to figure out whether or not someone is going to be a friend you can count on.

Here are six questions that you can ask yourself- and teach kids to ask themselves - to help decide whether or not someone is being a good friend.

1) Does this person do things that are important to both of you?
Or, does this person run hot and cold – acting glad to see you when she or he wants something from you, but getting mad and saying you are a bad friend if you want to do something else?

2) Does this person encourage you to do things that are in your best interests?
Or, does this person try to use your feelings of friendship to pressure you into wasting your time or money, breaking rules, getting into trouble, doing something dangerous, or hurting someone else?

3) Does this person speak and act respectfully towards you no matter who else is around?
Or, does this person sometimes make unkind jokes or ignore you in order to be popular with others?

4) Does this person try to tell the truth, apologize for mistakes, and keep

commitments most of the time?
Or, does this person blame others for his or her mistakes, lie, and break promises over and over?

5) Does this person treat others with kindness and respect?
Or, is this person cruel to some people – or nice to their faces and mean behind their backs? Remember that what someone does to someone else, sooner or later, this person is very likely to do to you.

6) Is this person willing to work problems out?
Or, does this person ignore problems and then explode or act ready to give up on the friendship as soon as something goes wrong?

The bottom line is that we all deserve to have healthy relationships in our lives and that healthy relationships take work. No matter how friendly someone acts and no matter how much we might like to be with this person, we need to decide whether this person is behaving in a way that is that is going to make our lives better or worse.

Suppose that you decide that someone you often enjoy is also often not acting like a good friend. Depending on the situation, here are some choices for what you can do:

1) Speak up about the problem in a clear, respectful way.
People often don't see the impact of their behavior on others unless it's pointed out to them. You can't know what will happen unless you let this person know that this behavior is not okay with you.

2) Become unavailable.
You can decide to spend your attention and time with someone else. Many shy people do not act that friendly at first, but, once you get past the surface, can be interesting and fun.

3) Pick and choose.
Many people are great to be with at some times and best to avoid at other times. You can decide when to hang out with someone and when not to.

4) End the friendship.
Sometimes the only way to end a friendship is to tell yourself that the friendship is over. Usually just being unavailable works, especially if you've tried to solve the problem and that didn't work. But once in a while, you might need to say something like, "I really appreciate the fun times we've had, but I've decided that it won't work for me to stay friends with you. I wish you very well and hope for the best for you, but won't be spending time with you any more."

Strong, true friendships make life rich and joyful. They give lasting memories, provide strength and comfort during difficult times, and help both friends to grow and to have fun. They deserve time, attention, and effort. But, that effort should help everyone grow stronger and closer. We can help young people build strong, meaningful friendships by making healthy decisions about who our own friends are and by encouraging them to choose – and to tend – their own friendships kindly and thoughtfully.

Strong, true friendships make life rich and joyful. They give lasting memories, provide strength and comfort during difficult times, and help both friends to grow and to have fun.

Clear communication is essential for healthy relationships.

Chapter Eighteen
Building Strong "People Safety" Skills

Assertive Advocacy
Teaching Children the Skill of Confidence
Teaching Children to Persist
The Power of Positive Practice
How to Pick a Good Self-Defense Program

Assertive Advocacy
How We Communicate is as Important as *What* We Communicate

Being able to advocate effectively for yourself and others is essential to taking charge effectively when dealing with bullying problems.

The word "advocacy" is used to mean "actively speaking up for yourself and others." Kidpower teaches Assertive Advocacy to people of all ages and abilities so that they are effective in:
• Setting boundaries
• Getting others to listen to them
• Asking for help
• Being included

I have heard children as young as five and adults as old as ninety complain that the personal safety skills that Kidpower taught them didn't work.

They might mumble passively, "I kind of tried what you told me, sort of anyway, and nobody listened. I don't know why. I guess that they just don't like me."

They might grump aggressively, "I did *exactly* what you said and NOBODY CARED ABOUT ME! They just got mad. I think they hate me, the creeps!"

How we communicate about what we do and do not want is going to make a huge difference in the results we are most likely to have. We can say all the right words, but this often won't work well unless we communicate our boundaries and wishes with an assertive attitude.

The difference between being passive, aggressive, and assertive can be learned at a young age – in fact, as soon as children can speak and understand language fairly well. In Kidpower workshops, we show children the difference with puppets, stories, and role-plays – and then coach them to try out different attitudes themselves.

When we act passively, the message that we communicate to others is, "What I want is not that important, and no one cares anyway, so I might as well give up." Our listeners are likely to agree with us – that our message must not be that important in the midst of so many other things competing much more persuasively for their attention. People will often fail to notice our message, will ignore it, or will forget it.

Examples of Passive Behavior
• A soft, unsure voice
• A hopeless expression
• Limp or frozen posture and gestures
• Eyes that are looking down or to the side so that there is no eye contact
• An apologetic or whiny tone of voice
• A closed down body that doesn't take up too much space
• Speaking from a bit too far away to be noticed
• Waiting and wishing that someone would just know what you want
• Sighing or shrugging
• Hesitant, unclear language

When we act aggressively, the message that we communicate to others is, "You are not going do what I want anyway, and you are probably out to get me, so I am mad at you. You are an awful person." Our listeners are likely to feel attacked and to believe that any message delivered in such a negative way is probably unreasonable. They might avoid us or get angry back.

Examples of Aggressive Behavior
• A glowering face
• A tense, rigid posture
• An irritated or loud voice
• Jabbing or jerky body language and gestures
• Strutting
• Insulting language and loaded words
• Leaning forward into someone's face
• Crowding into the space of others
• Interrupting others impatiently
• Not listening
• Acting annoyed or angry

Whining can somehow be both passive and aggressive. Sometimes, in Kidpower classes, we explore this with children. We ask them to use a very whiny voice and say words that would be relevant to their lives: "Teeeeecherrrr! Moooooooom! Daaaaaaaad! Noooooooooooooooooo! Stoooooooop! That's not faaaaaaaair! Coooooome ooooooooon! Pleeeeeeease!"

We then ask some leading questions to reinforce our point: "Does that sound like WHINING? Is it IRRITATING? I don't even feel like listening to myself! Do you feel like listening to yourself?"

Instead of communicating with either a passive or an aggressive attitude, both youth and adults can learn how to communicate assertively. Assertive Advocacy means giving others the message that, "Of course you are going to care about what I want once you understand what it is. What I have to say is very important to me, and I believe that you are such a good person that this will be very important to you too."

Having a positive, confident attitude makes life more fun!

Behavior that Communicates an Assertive Attitude
• Using body language that is calm, aware, and confident

• Making eye contact - When you want people to listen to you, it usually works best to look into their eyes without staring rudely and without looking away.

• Having a facial expression that is consistent with your message -This means having a neutral face if you are telling someone to stop or a friendly face if you are asking someone to do something for you.

• Using polite language that is both definite and respectful, such as, "Excuse me!" "Please stop!" "I need your help!" "I'd like to sit here, too." "I'd like to join the game."

• Making your voice loud enough to be easily heard and positive instead of soft, hesitant, whiny, or angry

• Sounding firm to tell someone to stop

• Sounding appreciative if you want help

• Sounding cheerful if you want someone to do something for you or with you

• Managing space - Move away from someone who you want to stop bothering you. Move closer to someone who you want something from.

Another pitfall to avoid is the Wishing Technique. Have you ever WISHED passively that someone would just know what you want without your having to say anything? Did it work? Did you ever give up and not get what you needed from that person? Did you ever become so frustrated that you blew up at that person aggressively?

Children might need adult help to learn that the Wishing Technique doesn't work most of the time. Children often believe that adults can read their minds. This is logical from a child's perspective, because, especially when children are younger, adults DO anticipate many of children's needs without them saying anything.

Remind children (and yourself) that, "It's not fair to give up on people or to get mad at them just because they cannot read your mind. This is why you need to use Assertive Advocacy to speak up for what you do want and what you do not want."

Most of the adults I know, including myself, will admit to using the Wishing Technique at times or to being passive or aggressive. Remember that the children in your life are learning from the example you set. Model Assertive Advocacy by being both strong and respectful in your communications - and coach children to do the same.

Teaching Children the Skill of Confidence
Having a confident attitude and having the confidence to set boundaries and

get help are tremendously useful skills when a young person faces bullying.

Sometimes people ask me, "Why do you keep saying that Kidpower teaches confidence? I think of confidence as meaning that you believe in yourself, and that's a feeling or a belief, not a skill that is taught!"

The reality is that confidence can be many things – a feeling, an attitude, a belief, a decision, and a set of skills that can be learned.

The feeling of confidence comes from believing that we are powerful, valuable, and competent. Some lucky people seem to feel confident just naturally most of the time. However, in working with thousands of students from all walks of life, we have found that people of all ages and abilities can learn to develop the skill of Showing Confidence, no matter how they feel inside.

We tell our students that, "People will listen to you better and bother you less if you Act Aware, Calm, and Confident." We then coach our students to practice sitting, talking, and walking while they Act Aware, Calm, and Confident by:

- Making their bodies tall and open with their shoulders down, their backs straight, and their heads up
- Using a "soft eye" as they look around rather than glaring at someone or acting timid
- Keeping a calm look on their faces and calm, strong body language
- Using a "regular voice" loud enough to be heard easily
- Speaking up about what they do and don't want using clear polite words
- Staying centered while the teacher pretends to be someone acting rude or scary

People can also learn the skills necessary to protect themselves from most experiences that can damage their feelings of confidence, to deal with problems in a way that develops their feelings of confidence, and to create experiences that will build their feelings of confidence.

One of my favorite insights from Stephen R. Covey's book *The 7 Habits of Highly Effective People* is that love is not just a feeling; loving someone is actually a decision. You can show love to another person if you have decided to love that person, even when you don't feel love towards that person at that moment. By doing so, you can often create the conditions that will lead more feelings of love between you and this person. (Making Safe Decisions About Love and Showing Love in Healthy Ways are also skills that we can learn, but that's a different book.)

The same principle is true with confidence. Acting with a lack of confidence is likely to cause you to doubt yourself even more and to cause others to treat you with less interest and respect, which often leads to your having experiences that can increase your feelings of doubting yourself, creating a downward spiral leading to more loss of confidence. Instead, you can learn how to show confidence and decide to use this skill no matter how you feel inside. By doing so, you are more likely to to have experiences that will cause your confidence to grow.

You can learn how to show confidence and decide to use this skill no matter how you feel inside.

Getting little kids to hike up big mountains.

Teaching Children to Persist
What Does Persistence Have To Do with Stopping Bullying?
Too often, children don't get help when they are being bullied because they get discouraged by busy, impatient adults.

Although in Kidpower we know how to make learning People Safety skills easy for our students, actually using these skills out in the real world is often frustrating and difficult. For example, setting a boundary in the face of peer disapproval can be uncomfortable, and persisting in getting help when no one seems to be listening can be very hard work. In order for children to trust in their personal power, they need to know how to keep going even when they feel upset, discouraged, unhappy, embarrassed, or tired.

What Adults Can Do
Adults can support the development of persistence in the following ways:
• Give children opportunities to take on challenges where they can be successful;
• Offer guidance rather than taking over for them when children ask for help;
• Acknowledge unhappy feelings without letting children give up on themselves;
• Break a challenge into smaller steps when children get stuck; and,
• Motivate children to keep going even when they don't feel like it.

Getting Little Kids To Hike Up Big Mountains
Physical activities can help build confidence in the ability to keep going. Some people do this through sports or dance. When my own kids were young, I would do it through hikes and camping trips with our family, our Girl Scout troop, and our Campfire Boy's group. My theory was that, no matter what they said, if the children with me had energy enough to run around, yell, or splash in streams once we sat down during a hike, they had energy enough to keep on going.

"But I'm too tired! I can't!" the children often complained. "It's too far!"
"I understand," I would say cheerfully. "Just keep putting one foot in front of the other and you'll make it to the top. I promise."

Sometimes our hikes took longer and included a bit of moaning and groaning, but we always got there. I offered motivators to help make the hike more interesting and fun. Conversation. Undivided attention. Treats for the trail. Stories. Songs.

When children were really resistant, I upped the ante. "I love you too much to let you give up!" I explained to one young Girl Scout. For two miles, I held her sweaty hand firmly in my own to keep her from falling, since she insisted on staggering dramatically to show both of us (and everybody watching) how exhausted she was. When we got to the part of the trail that involved climbing over rocks with handholds, this girl got interested and excitedly joined her friends.

I encouraged the children hiking with me not to complain and did my best to reward cheerful perseverance. Their sense of accomplishment at the end of the trail always made whatever struggles we had along the way worth the work.

Persistence Pays

Recent research shows that children who were praised for trying hard did better on intelligence tests than children who were just told that they were smart. The reason seems to be that children who were just told that they were smart were afraid of failure. Children who understood that their brains are like muscles that need exercise were more likely to take risks and to expend effort. Expending effort in the face of inner discomfort and outer discouragement takes work. Learning how to persist is a skill that can serve children well, not only in being safe with people, but in all areas of their lives.

The Power of Positive Practice

Whether you are preparing to advocate for your child to deal with a bullying problem or preparing children to set boundaries for themselves, rehearsing what to do can make a huge difference in your confidence and effectiveness.

Many studies show that just raising awareness of problems and worrying about them raises anxiety. However, having opportunities for successful practice of skills for dealing with different problems helps people become more confident, less anxious, and more effective.

Rehearsing what to do can prepare people to handle many difficult situations related to personal safety. For example, practice can help you and the people important to you prepare to:

• Make new friends the first day of school;
• Set a boundary with someone who is not being respectful;
• Be persistent in getting help from someone who is busy and overwhelmed;
• Stay safe emotionally when someone is being hurtful;
• Leave a threatening situation in a peaceful, powerful way;
• In an emergency, use self-defense skills to stop an attack;

In addition, rehearsal is useful in preparing to handle other important skills such as to conduct a job interview; change a tire; take appropriate action in an earthquake or a snowstorm; and learn a new computer skill.

HOW someone practices is as important as the practice itself. Practicing doing something wrong can make you and others less effective. Practicing in ways that leave you feeling like a failure can be destructive to your belief in yourself and can harm your self-esteem.

You can set up safe, positive practices for yourself and others by remembering these key components of the Kidpower Positive Practice Teaching Method:

1. Stay Calm. No matter how difficult or upsetting the issue is, you and anyone you are trying to help will learn better if you are calm.

2. Overcome Resistance. People often try to avoid practicing how to handle a situation because they would rather just talk about it or because thinking about it is upsetting. Sometimes people are afraid they will look stupid if they practice. While talking can be helpful to build understanding, most people need to practice a skill in order to become better at it.

Most people need to practice a skill in order to become better at it.

Having opportunities for successful practice can help kids to become more confident and less anxious.

3. Know What You Want to Accomplish. Learn about the best ways to handle situations from others through reading, watching videos, asking people who have experience, or taking workshops. Become clear about what you want the outcome to be and what you or others need to be able to do or to say to make it happen.

4. If you are teaching someone else, be competent yourself. For example, if you cannot sound and look clear, respectful, and firm when you set a boundary, modeling this effectively for someone else is going to be difficult. One of the great benefits of showing others what to do is that you can become better at using this skill yourself.

5. Be Specific. To create a role-play, be specific about who the parties involved are, where you are, what the problem is, and what the technique is. You can practice by yourself out loud in front of a mirror or with other people. Adjust and adapt for differences in how you can best respond, including the different life situations of the people you might be wanting to communicate with or about.

6. Use Your Imagination. For problems that are not possible to practice in the actual situation, you can prepare yourself by visualizing different problems and imagining step by step what you are going to do. If you want to practice something with children, remember that kids are used to playing games with imaginary props and characters. All you have to do is be clear on who is who and what is what and where is where. If you are practicing with people who have trouble visualizing or generalizing, use props or drawings and make what you are doing as context-specific as possible.

7. Make It Successful. When you or others take on a role, remember you are just pretending for the purpose of practice. This is not a test for you or anyone else. To ensure success, go step-by-step and get or give coaching so that the people involved are rewarded with accomplishment each step of the way. People often need to be walked through a practice several times before being able to do it effectively. Remember that a good play, for example, takes repeated rehearsal.

8. Get Coaching and Feedback. Often very minor details that you might not be aware of can make a huge impact on your effectiveness. One small step that you don't know or forget to do can make a large difference in dealing with anything technological – like not saving a document regularly when using your computer. With communication skills, ask for feedback and coaching on the most effective choice of words, tone of voice, facial expressions, and body language.

9. Write Things Down. If you have a hard time remembering what to do, write the steps and ideas down as specifically as possible. Writing often helps people to integrate what they want to learn. Try using the written steps to practice the skill. Post reminders for anything that you want to remember or change.

10. Remember that Mistakes Are Part of Learning. Look for progress, not perfection. Give yourself and others the time to learn. People are far more likely to accept practicing if they are being encouraged rather than criticized.

Be patient with yourself and with anyone who you are trying to teach. If someone feels upset about making a mistake, say something encouraging like, "This is hard to do. That is why we practice." Remember that, "You do not have to be perfect to be great."

11. Be Sensitive to Different Ages and Life Situations. Err on the side of safety in terms of what you decide to say to children. Remember that even though some children might sound knowledgeable or even quite cynical, they vary widely in their degree of actual sophistication. Make sure that your examples and directions are relevant for the people you are teaching. For example, don't tell someone in a wheelchair to stand up, and don't tell a teen boy to imagine that you have stolen his favorite doll.

12. Stay Respectful. To make sure that practicing stays emotionally safe, don't allow putdowns or teasing or generalizations that are prejudicial unless your practices themselves are about building skills to be safe from these kinds of comments.

13. Stay Positive. Remember to focus on what you want yourself or others to do to be safe and NOT discuss or imagine all the scary things that might happen. If you are leading a practice, be sure that your tone of voice, facial expressions, body language, and choice of words convey enthusiasm.

14. Walk Your Talk. If you are teaching respect and responsibility to others, be sure that you are modeling this behavior yourself. For example, if you make putdown jokes, use sarcastic humor or chronically miss commitments like being on time, don't be surprised if your students, children, or employees do the same.

How To Choose a Good Self-Defense Program
The right kind of self-defense program can help young people to develop both confidence and skills to prevent and stop most bullying.

With any kind of class, the quality of the program and approach of the instructor will make a huge difference in the results. Self-defense is no exception. Done well, self-defense workshops can be exciting, empowering, and useful. Done poorly, they can be boring, discouraging, and destructive. If training is about self-defense or any other important life skills, the potential benefits are real and so are the potential problems.

In our Kidpower and Teenpower self-defense programs, we give young people the opportunity to practice skills for protecting their emotional and physical safety with peers, known adults, and strangers. The following questions to consider when evaluating any self-defense program are based on our over 20 years of experience with thousands of students of all ages and abilities.

1. Is the content positive, accurate, comprehensive, and appropriate for the ages and life situations of the students?
The best programs will teach a range of personal safety skills for being aware, taking charge of the space around you, getting help, setting boundaries with people you know, de-escalating conflict, and staying calm

In a good self-defense program, physical self-defense skills will be taught in a context of having done everything possible to get out of a situation safely without fighting first.

and making choices instead of just getting upset when you have a problem. Physical self-defense skills will be taught in a context of having done everything possible to get out of a situation safely without fighting first.

Look for programs that focus on the skills to learn rather than on reasons why we have to learn these skills. Realize that children can become traumatized by scary stories about bad things that happened to other children. Children learn best if their teacher has a calm, matter-of-fact approach which makes it clear that they can keep themselves safe most of the time by learning how to do a few easy things.

Look for programs that are based on research from a wide variety of fields including mental health, education, crime prevention, law enforcement, and martial arts.

Look for endorsements from real people and credible organizations.

Look for programs that are willing to give credit for what they have learned from others rather than saying that they have invented "the best and only way to learning true self-defense."

Be wary of programs that give simplistic, absolute answers such as, "If you wear a pony tail, you are very likely to be assaulted" or "If you train with us, you will never have to be afraid again."

2. Is the teacher clear, respectful, in charge, enthusiastic, and able to adapt?
You and the children and teens in your life deserve to have teachers who are helpful rather than discouraging. Good teachers do not make negative remarks about their students or anyone else and do not allow others to do so, even as a joke.

Look for teachers who know how to be both firm and respectful when they set boundaries with students who are doing things that detract from the class.

The best teachers will change what they do to meet the needs of their students rather than having a standard, canned approach. Role-plays to demonstrate or practice skills should be described in terms of situations that students are likely to encounter. The way something is presented should be in terms that are meaningful to a student. Instead of telling a blind student to look at a potential attacker, for example, a teacher who knows how to adapt will say something like, "Turn your face towards the person so that he knows you know he's there."

Good teachers will listen to your concerns with appreciation for your having the courage to raise them rather than with defensiveness. When possible, they will change what they do to make the class work better for you. At the very least, they will explain their reasons for what they do and why they cannot accommodate your wishes.

3. Is the approach more action-oriented or talking-oriented?
In general, people remember more about what they have seen than what they have been told. People are more likely to be able to do what they have

practiced themselves than what they have been shown to do or told to do.

Look for programs that involve showing more than explaining and that provide lots of opportunity for learning by doing.

4. Is the learning success-based?
It can be destructive to students' emotional and physical safety if they feel as if they are failing when they are trying to learn self-protection skills. Success-based learning means that students are guided through what they need to learn in a highly positive way. Practices go step by step starting with where each student actually is. Success is defined as progress for each individual student rather than as perfection according to some standard of the teacher. Students are coached as they do the practices so that they can do them correctly as much as possible. They are given feedback about how to improve in a context that communicates, "mistakes are part of learning."

5. Is the approach more focused on traditional martial arts or on practical self-defense?
Martial arts programs, like other activities involving interactive movement such as sports and dance, can be wonderful for building confidence, character, and physical condition. However, for teaching personal safety skills, the approach of most martial arts is like long-term preventative health care. Practical self-defense is like emergency medicine, which teaches in a few hours skills that are very focused on preventing abduction, assault, and abuse from strangers, bullies, and people we know.

The most important skill in choosing a good self-defense program is being able to act on your intuition without being stopped by feelings of confusion or fear. It can be hard to stay clear about what your needs are or what the needs of your children are when you are bombarded by often conflicting advice from experts. If something someone does seems wrong to you, even if you can't justify your feeling logically, walk away rather than staying in a potentially bad situation. Keep looking until you find the type of program that answers to your satisfaction the kinds of questions described above.

Whether you are looking for a self-defense class or any other important training, pay attention to uncomfortable feelings you have about someone's approach, no matter how highly-recommended the person is and no matter how much you like the teacher as a person. Often very well meaning, knowledgeable people try to teach through talking about what can go wrong rather than through helping their students practice how to do things effectively. Remember that what programs actually do is more important than what their literature or representatives say they are going to do. In Kidpower Teenpower Fullpower International, we do our best to uphold high standards for all of our services. Please let us know if ever we do not follow through on this commitment.

How to Teach the Famous Kidpower Trash Can
In over twenty years of self-defense work, the Kidpower Trash Can is the technique I personally use the most. At first, we just taught this to little children, but then we found that, as self-defense instructors, we were using

If something someone does seems wrong to you, even if you can't justify your feeling logically, walk away rather than staying in a potentially bad situation.

The Kidpower Trash Can works for all ages.

the Kidpower Trash Can ourselves, so we started teaching it to everybody.

The concept is quite simple. You *catch* hurting words, *throw* them into the trash and *put* something nice that you say aloud into yourself. Of course, you can do this with your imagination by using your mind, but there is something very powerful about practicing out loud and using your body. Also, practicing in this way helps you remember to protect yourself from hurting words out in the real world.

Sometimes we start by having younger children catch the word "Stupid" by grabbing with their hands to make "Mean Word Catchers."

Next, we all throw the word "Stupid" towards a real trash can. I explain that everybody has perfect catch and perfect aim in Kidpower. Finally, we all pat our chests while we say the nice words that can replace the hurtful ones, in this case, "I'm *smart*!"

You can also use your body to make a Kidpower Trash Can. Put a hand on one of your hips. Imagine that the hole made by your arm is the top of a trash can. When people say mean things to you, you can catch the hurting words with your free hand and throw them into the hole made by your other arm. Finally, you can pat your chest while you say something good to yourself.

One little boy who was just two-and-a-half was getting teased at a birthday party because he had a cast. His mother saw him make his Kidpower Trash Can and shout, "NO! I am not letting your hurting words go inside my body!"

After the Kidpower program has been in a school, teachers tell us they see younger kids on the playground, hands on their hips, throwing away hurtful words, and saying, "I like myself!"

Preparing to Use Your Imagination Trash Can
Of course, going around in public turning their bodies into trash cans and saying nice things to themselves out loud would not be a good idea for older children. In fact, most the time, the safest thing for young people to do in a confrontation with peers is to protect themselves emotionally, perhaps by using a trash can in their minds, while they leave silently.

We have countless stories of how people of all ages have found that using the Kidpower Trash Can either at the time or later, either for real or in their imaginations, helped them take the power out of upsetting words.

As Patrick's mother told us, "At age eleven, Patrick would get outraged when teens on the way home from school would say rude things about his disabled sister. His need to answer them back instead of leaving was putting both Patrick and his sister in danger.

"We practiced with each insult that had upset Patrick. We said the words aloud sneering and gesturing while Patrick walked away and used his Kidpower Trash Can. Each time, he would say out loud, 'My sister is great.' We had his sister practice too. We told them both that answering people on the street would not be safe, but that taking the power out of these words would help them to stay calm, aware, and confident. Instead of dreading the walk home from school, they started enjoying their independence. When Patrick stopped reacting, the boys left them alone."

Older children sometimes appreciate having an intellectual connection to make the Trash Can Technique seem more relevant to them. Catching the trash helps you react with your brain first, not with your feelings. Throwing it away represents assessing the situation and deciding what to do to make things better. Finally, telling yourself something positive and taking it in is a way of taking care of yourself, just as you might wash your hands after picking up something dirty.

A Word of Warning

Sometimes people are surprised that children will misuse the Trash Can Technique, either accidentally or because they are testing boundaries.

During a teacher training at a preschool, one of the teachers said that she had shown her children the Kidpower Trash Can Technique.

Later that week on the playground, when one girl complained that another child had called her a name, the teacher said, "So, do you remember what to do?"

With perfect confidence, this three-year-old said, "Yes I do!" She put her hand on her hip to make a Kidpower Trash Can and then used her other hand to grab the shirt of the girl who was bothering her, with a clear intention of throwing *her* away.

When children are experimenting with new tools, adults need to be prepared to step in if need be. One way to think about this is to compare it to giving a young child a pair of scissors for the first time. What would happen if you just showed the child how to cut with the scissors and then left the room? A curious child might start cutting the curtains or someone's hair or try flushing the scissors down the toilet to see what happens. Children need supervision when they get new tools of any kind until they show that they know how to use these tools safely.

Long Spaghetti: A Successful Practice for Taking the Power Out of Loaded Words

Things that might seem silly to adults can humiliate a young person. In one of our classes, a fourteen-year-old boy was mortified because, since he was growing tall so quickly, other kids were calling him "long spaghetti."

These words had become so loaded for him that he had to watch the Kidpower teachers practice throwing away the words "long spaghetti" with each other before he could practice for himself. His parents said later that just doing this simple exercise changed his whole attitude about going to school.

The Mini-Trash Can

The ten-year-old daughter of one of our instructors arrived home upset every day. When she rode the school bus, other kids kept calling her "tree stump" because she was short. She felt too old to use the trash can the way she'd practiced, but just using her imagination wasn't enough. So she and her mother invented a mini-trash can that she could use behind her back so the other kids wouldn't see it.

The next day, the girl came flying into the house shouting, "It worked! It worked! When they called me 'tree stump,' I made my little trash can. They asked me what I was doing, and I told them I was putting their words into my mini-trash can. They got so interested that they forgot all about teasing me."

To make a mini-trash can, curl up the fingers of one hand against your palm to make a hole and use your thumb to push words onto the top of the hole.

Foul Language

Often, the words that upset children are "bad words" they are not allowed to say. In some classes with pre-teens or teens, with permission from parents and teachers, we practice having young people throw away these specific words in order to take the power out of them. We explain that these words are just a set of sounds, and their bad meanings came from people, not from the sounds themselves. In different languages, the "bad words" often sound completely different. You do not want a set of sounds to control how you feel or what you decide to do.

Unless we have permission, we never use foul language in Kidpower children's programs. This is partly because families have very different tolerance about "bad words" and also because we do not want to teach children hurtful words that they have not already heard. Instead we tell children, "I want you to think of the *worst* words you can think of for someone to call you! ... *Do NOT* say these words out loud! ... Suppose that I say, 'You're nothing but a *Really Bad Word*,' or '*Bleep*!' You can imagine that I said the words you were thinking of and throw those words away. Then you can tell yourself, 'I'm proud of who I am!'"

Recycling

Recycling garbage rather than throwing it into a landfill is better for the earth. Once children really understand the concept of not taking hurting words inside or of littering the world with them, I will say, "Recycling trash like paper or compost trash like orange peels is important. If you think about it, what we are actually doing is *recycling* the mean words after we throw them away, by breaking them down into their letters and turning them into nice words. Like compost can be used to fertilize plants, the nice words we tell ourselves can help us to grow stronger."

Practicing Using the Kidpower Trash Can

1. We are very careful about how we practice using the Trash Can. We do not want children to be harmed by taking in some hurtful words accidentally through the practice. We make this emotionally safe by:

• Saying very clearly, "I am just pretending so we can practice." If this is a young child or someone who might get confused, we say this *each time* we practice.

• Making sure that the child has the answer ready *before* we say the hurting words.

- Letting the child choose the words to throw away as much as possible. Ask, "Is there anything hurtful that other people say to you or that you say to yourself that you want to practice throwing away?

- Using words that the child has already heard rather than introducing new insults.

- Picking something the child can change unless the child has asked us to pick something personal. For example, we will not say, "You have an ugly nose!" Instead, we will say, "That's an ugly shirt." Or we might say something generic like, "*Shut up!*"

- Letting the child decide which kind of trash can to use – a real one nearby, the arm on the hip, the mini-trash can, or some other variation such as the one-handed trash can (just waving the words away with one arm), a dumpster (two mini-trash-cans next to each other), etc. Children sometimes have fun making up their own trash cans. Make sure that the child's trash can of choice is ready for action before you say anything.

2. To practice, agree on the insult, affirmation, and method of trash can to be used. You say the insult out loud. The child physically catches the insult and throws it away. Next, the child uses an affirmation to say something nice to herself or himself and physically takes this in, perhaps by patting her or his chest while saying it. The list below gives you some ideas, but keep the guidelines described above in mind when deciding which to use.

Insult: "You're ugly." Or, "You look nice – *Not!*"

Affirmation: "I like the way I look." Or, "I have my own way of looking good."

Insult: "SHUT UP!"
Affirmation: "My words are important."

Insult: "You're lazy."
Affirmation: "I am relaxed, and I enjoy myself."

Insult: "I don't want to sit next to you. You smell!"
Affirmation: "I can find another place to sit. I'm proud of who I am."

Insult: "I don't want to play with you."
Affirmation: "I will find another friend."

Insult: "Duh!" Or, "That sucks!"
Affirmation: "I have the right to my own opinion."

Insult: "Crybaby!"
Affirmation: "Everybody cries. Adults too. It's healthy."

Insult: "Your food looks weird!" Or, "That's a dumb shirt."
Affirmation: " I like my food!" Or, "I like my shirt."

Insult: "How could you make such an awful mistake?"
Affirmation: "Mistakes are part of learning." Or, with a shrug, "Nobody's perfect!" Or, "You don't have to be perfect to be great!"

Insult: "I hate you!"
Affirmation: "I love myself!"

Insult: (to a child wearing glasses) "Four eyes!"
Affirmation: "I like my glasses. They help me see!"

Insult: "You're not trying hard enough." Or, "You're not getting enough done."
Affirmation: "I do the best I can and I do *a lot*."

3. If a child is being taunted by foul language, we recommend practicing with the specific words the tormentors are using, even if it makes the adults leading the practice uncomfortable to say these words out loud. If a child is too upset to have the words directed to her or him, then you can start by having adults or stuffed animals practicing with each other to demonstrate. Again, be clear that *we are pretending so we can practice*!

4. Sometimes older children resist practicing because it seems too childish. Adults can acknowledge their reality by saying, "Of course you won't do this out in the school yard. But practicing with me will help you to remember the Trash Can as a metaphor, or a picture for your mind, when you need it. You can say something positive to yourself silently instead of out loud. If you don't like the Trash Can image, what are some other ideas you have for how to dispose of hurting words instead of taking them inside?"

Chapter Nineteen

Tools for Creating a United Front Against Bullying

Sample Bullying, Harassment, and Violence Prevention Proclamation
Sample School Action Plan
Sample School Policies
An Opportunity to Grow

The safety of kids is everybody's business. When adults work together to address and stop harmful behavior, our families, schools, organizations, social groups, places of worship, and workplaces can become safer, more joyful, and more effective in achieving their goals.

As adults, we are responsible for taking a strong stand against bullying, harassment, and other kinds of emotional and physical violence in any place where we leave our kids. In order to create a shared vision and implement a practical reality, a group or institution can:

Agree on a written public proclamation that declares this institution or group's commitment to promoting a culture of caring, safety, and respect for all its members;

Establish a written plan of action that involves everyone within this institution or group - children, parents, teachers, administrators, etc. - and that provides skills and support for implementing this plan.

Establish and uphold written policies about what the requirements are and how they will be upheld.

The following tools are also available on our website so that they can be used as the basis of creating your own Proclamation, Action Plan, and Policies.

Cooperation Power.

Sample Bullying, Harassment, and Violence Prevention Proclamation

We agree that:

People of all ages and abilities have the right to be safe from physical and emotional attack.

Any form of behavior that is threatening, harassing, bullying, or dangerous must be stopped.
Families, schools, colleges, organizations, workplaces, places of worship, and other groups are responsible for empowering and protecting their members and for promoting cultures of caring, respect, and safety for everyone.

Adults are responsible for taking leadership to ensure that bullying, harassment and other forms of violence and abuse are clearly against the rules, that everyone understands the rules, and that these rules are upheld. Mechanisms that are clearly understood by everyone need to be in place to deal with problems that come up in a prompt, fair, open, and effective fashion.

Everyone in a position of leadership is responsible for modeling consistent, powerful, and respectful behavior – and for intervening to address unsafe behavior.

People who feel threatened, upset, or endangered by someone's behavior – or who see this happening to someone else - have both the right and the responsibility to speak up. They have the responsibility for behaving in ways that are safe and respectful to others.

Most people are empowered when they know how to take charge of their own safety, how to act safely towards others even if they feel frustrated or upset, how to intervene, and how to advocate effectively.

People of all ages and abilities have the right to develop understanding and skills through high quality programs that give them the opportunity to be successful in practicing in contexts that are relevant to their lives.

We understand that:

this Proclamation is effective only when we each, individually, have the courage and determination to act in ways that reflect our commitment to these principles, especially in the face of embarrassment, inconvenience, and offense.

while children have great power to participate in building and supporting a culture of caring, community, and respect, the adults will retain full responsibility for the ultimate outcome and will provide the leadership and guidance necessary for maintaining an environment that is physically and emotionally safe for everyone in the community.

We will renew this proclamation annually, or more frequently if needed, in order to ensure our actions continue to reflect our commitment to these principles and to make changes as needed to ensure the safety of everyone in our community.

Sample School Action Plan

Adopt a Bullying, Harassment, and Violence Prevention Proclamation similar to the one above. Agreeing on a shared vision and commitment is essential in making lasting change.

Make sure that all school staff and families know what your vision and commitment are. Post the Proclamation on your website and include it in your school handbook.

Turn the Proclamation into specific policies about how problems are going to be handled. A sample School Policy is below.

At the beginning of each school year, send a letter home to parents with guidelines about how to talk with their children and the school's Bullying and Harassment Prevention Proclamation and Policies. Even younger children can be told, "We expect you to be safe at school. If anything ever happens that makes you feel unsafe or unhappy, we want you to go to a teacher for help right away and to tell us as soon as you can. We also expect you to act in ways that are safe and respectful to other people. If you or the school tells us that you have threatened or been disrespectful to someone, we will work together to help you figure out how to solve problems with people in other ways."

Have a discussion in the classroom each year about what the rules are. Use age-appropriate examples to help students understand what kinds of behavior are considered safe and unsafe, what their choices are about how to handle different kinds of problems, and what the consequences are for unsafe behavior.

Give students the opportunity to learn and practice "People Safety" skills of the kind taught by Kidpower, including how to avoid trouble, set boundaries, handle conflict, and ventilate upset feelings without using threatening or abusive language and without using physical violence. If they cannot handle problems on their own, give students practice in how to be persistent and respectful in getting adult help.

Give educators and parents training in how to supervise students to support the use of these "People Safety" skills; how to assess and intervene when problems are not being resolved in a safe way; and how to enforce clear consequences for unsafe behavior in a firm, respectful way.

If a serious incident occurs, have a plan to make sure that the student who came for help is protected from any threats or other repercussions. This usually means having very close supervision of all parties involved in the incident, including friends of the offending student, until everything is resolved. The parents of all students involved need to be contacted and met with by the school. Sometimes a counselor can be asked to facilitate a meeting to create a safe place to air feelings and then figure out how to use this incident as an opportunity to learn and grow.

When an upsetting event has occurred, the names of the students should be kept confidential as much as possible. However, to ensure emotional safety, all of the people in the school community who might hear about the incident need to be informed about what happened and about what steps are being taken to address the situation. Both teachers and parents can review the school's Proclamation and Policies with children in an age-appropriate way. If kids are talking about what happened, adults need to be given guidance in how to lead discussions that are clear and educational rather than scary.

Agree on consequences for unsafe behavior and ensure that these consequences are consistently enforced. At Kidpower, we recommend that an effective management tool to address times when children behave in rude, unkind, or destructive ways is to require all parties in the moment to practice skills for how they might handle the situation in a safer way.

Note: In a school where threats about weapons might be a concern, everyone needs to clearly understand what to do if a weapon is present. Students need to be told to get up and leave for a safer place right away if they see a weapon or hear someone talking about using one. They need to get help immediately from someone at the school and they need to tell their parents - and their identity must be protected.

If children are being threatened with a weapon, they are most likely to be safer if they to give the person threatening them whatever property that person wants, and calm the situation down by saying whatever the person wants them to say, even if it's very upsetting and untrue. (e.g. "You're right. I'm no good. My parents are no good. I won't tell.") Once they are safely out of the situation, they need to go to an adult they can trust to help and protect them and to stay with that or another adult until they are with their parents.

Sample School Bullying, Harassment, and Violence Prevention Policy

Our commitment is to ensuring an emotionally and physically safe environment in our school community. We will do our best to stop any behavior that is threatening, harassing, bullying, or dangerous. If any student, parent, or staff member feels threatened, upset, or endangered by someone's behavior, that person has both the right and the responsibility to speak up.

Our goal is to prevent problems whenever possible. We expect adults to supervise children at all times and to intervene in a firm, respectful way to stop unsafe behavior. We offer conflict resolution training and self-protection and boundary-setting training through our school community. We ask parents to discuss our expectations about safe behavior with their children.

We work hard to create an environment where children can feel safe and happy most of the time, but understand that being upset or afraid occasionally is a normal part of life. We are committed to giving children support and skills for talking about their feelings and for getting help when they need to. Even though all of us are busy, we want to encourage children to develop the habit of talking problems over with their parents and teachers. If they feel unhappy or unsafe, we don't want them to feel alone and we do want them to have adult help in figuring out what to do.

If a problem occurs, our focus is on addressing situations in ways that seek solutions rather than blame. We will do our best to deal with problems in a prompt, pro-active, fair, and effective fashion.

Most concerns about student behavior can be resolved on an individual level by talking with the teacher or yard duty teacher - or by speaking directly with the individuals involved. If this doesn't work or if a serious incident occurs, the following process will take place.
The teacher and the parents of the child or children involved will meet separately with the principal and/or school counselor. A plan will be made so that students will understand what happened and will get the counseling or other support they need to deal with whatever happened and to prevent future problems. Every effort will be made to protect students raising concerns from retaliation.

A letter will go home to parents in the classroom without naming the families involved. The letter will describe what happened and what steps were taken to address the situation. The letter will suggest how parents might talk with their children about what happened in an age appropriate positive way.

For a severe situation, a meeting will be held so parents can discuss their concerns and get help in how to talk to their children.

Where appropriate, training will be offered to the parents, teachers, and students involved in the incident.

If there is a concern involving the behavior of an adult working at the school, most of the time this issue can be resolved by speaking directly with that individual.

If this doesn't work, or if the adult's behavior raises concerns about the safety of the children or other people, the principal, vice principal and/or school counselor should be approached immediately with the concern. Prompt action will be taken to address the problem in a solution-oriented, fair, and pro-active fashion.

An Opportunity to Grow
Bullying can lead to great growth – as well as causing big problems. With clear boundaries, better skills, and strong support, everyone involved can learn what to do, as well as what not to do.

Conflict is a normal part of most relationships because people have different perspectives and priorities. While kids need adult supervision so that they learn how to deal with conflict constructively, most upsetting behavior between people is not bullying. Bullying means that someone is using a power imbalance with the deliberate intention of harming another person. People can also harass or be hurtful to each other because of thoughtlessness, annoyance, poor self control, or experimentation with negative uses of their power without realizing the impact.

The good news is that the social-emotional skills that can prevent and stop most bullying and harassment are also important in building healthy relationships.

As one mother wrote, "I look at what my son gained from the episode of his life when he got badly bullied and then was bullying for a short period of time himself (which led to our finding out about him being bullied), and I must say that he's so much better off now. It was not easy, it was not quick, but it taught all of us such a lot of good things. Because of the work we did together and the support we received, my son learned to make new friends. He became strong in himself and immune to peer pressure – the dream of every parent for a teenager!"

Learning how to take charge of their own safety, how to act safely towards others even if they feel frustrated or upset, and how to advocate effectively empowers most people and gives them tools to better manage future conflicts and relationship issues.

Introducing the
Kidpower Safety Signs

What are the Kidpower Safety Signs?

The problems of bullying, violence, and abuse can seem complex and confusing. Kidpower People Safety skills provide solutions. People Safety skills help people be emotionally and physically safe with people at school, at home, out in the world, online – everywhere. The Kidpower Safety Signs show core People Safety skills and concepts in their simplest forms. Parents, caregivers, and professionals use these signs, along with simple gestures and words, to teach powerful safety skills and concepts quickly and easily.

Thanks to a three-year grant from the Special Hope Foundation, the Kidpower Safety Signs were originally created to help teachers, family members, and other caregivers teach People Safety skills and concepts to people with developmental disabilities who have limited speech – or no speech at all. Since their creation, the Safety Signs have proven useful to many people who want an easy way to remember key People Safety concepts - including people with developmental disabilities, young children, college students, and corporate managers. Kidpower Safety Signs are useful for everyone, everywhere!

Four Keys to Learning Safety Skills

Bullying, abuse, and other violence are crucial health issues of our time. The good news is that a few simple People Safety skills can stop most problems before they get dangerous. Thousands of people of all ages and abilities have learned and used these skills to be safe.

For everyone, the four keys to success in learning important safety skills are:
• Simplicity - because simple things are easier to remember
• Consistency - because consistent messages make more sense
• Repetition - because successful practice makes skills stronger
• Relevance - because people learn a skill faster when it seems useful

These keys are even more important for individuals who tend to think in concrete, simple terms, such as young children and people with developmental disabilities. Family members, teachers, and professionals will often use highly varying words and ideas to explain about safety, which can be confusing. Kidpower Safety Signs help everyone be clear, accurate, and consistent so that skills develop more effectively. They create a common language that makes it easy and fun for everyone, everywhere, to use the same words, gestures, and ideas about staying safe with people.

Teaching and Learning the Kidpower Safety Signs

Please review the signs on the following pages before teaching them to others and practice the signs in the air to help you feel comfortable with the movements. Then, teach the signs to your children or students acting them out together. Help put the signs into context by practicing them in simple situations. For example, say, "When you feel like you are getting upset, use your Calm Down Power (do the Safety Sign together) to help you stay calm so you can make safer choices." Remember that repetition is key to learning any new skill, so keep practicing until you feel your student has integrated the sign, and then continue practicing when new situations arise.

Kidpower Safety Powers for Taking Charge of Your Feelings and Your Body

If We Feel Upset, We Can Use These Safety Powers.

1.Calm Down Power

TAKE A BREATH

STRAIGHTEN YOUR BACK

2. Mouth Closed Power

3. Hands and Feet Down Power

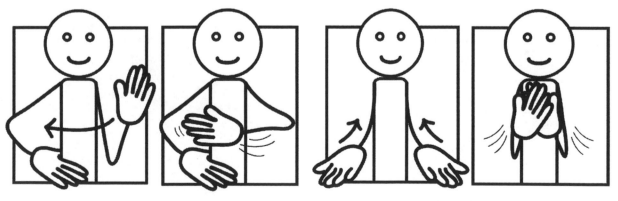

4. Trash Can Power

5. Heart Power

Kidpower Safety Powers for Building Better Relationships

We can have more fun and less problems with people when we use these Safety Powers

1. Listening Power

2. Speak Up Power

3. No, Thank You Power

4. Cooperation Power

5. Appreciation Power
(Hooray Power)

Kidpower Safety Sign Powers for Taking Charge of Your Safety

If someone is acting in a way that feels unsafe, we can make safer choices using these Safety Powers.

1. Awareness Power

2. Stop Power

3. Walk Away Power

3. Roll Away Power
   if you are on wheels

4. Go Get Help Power

Kidpower Boundaries on Touch and Teasing Safety Signs

Touch, play, or games for fun, teasing, or affection should be safe, okay with each person, allowed by the adults in charge, and not a secret, which means that everyone can know about it.

1. Safe

2. Okay with Each Person

3. Allowed by the adults in charge

4. Everyone Can Know

Kidpower's Boundaries Rules:

1. **We each belong to ourselves**

2. **Some things are not a choice**

3. **Problems should not be secrets**

4. **Keep telling until you get help**

Kidpower Safety Plan Signals

This is our Safety Plan when we go out

1. We Stay Aware

2. We Stay Together

3. We Check First with the adults in charge

4. We Think First

5. We Move Away

2. We Get Help (find Safety)

Other Resources From Kidpower

Workshops and Coaching for Families, Schools, and Organizations

In our Centers, we offer a wide range of public and privately organized workshops that use our Positive Practice teaching method to give our students the opportunity to learn and practice boundary-setting, awareness, conflict resolution, self-protection, and self-defense skills in contexts relevant to their lives. Our full-force programs include practice of self-defense techniques with a head-to-toe padded instructor.

Services include: Kidpower Parent/Caregiver Education, Kidpower Parent-Child workshops, teacher training, Kidpower self-defense workshops, Teenpower self-defense workshops, Fullpower self-defense for adults, classroom programs, programs for people with special needs, and workplace communication and violence prevention programs.

One-time or ongoing coaching sessions can be tailored to fit your specific needs. These can be conducted anywhere by Skype or telephone. Contact us at safety@kidpower.org or visit our website to see our locations and learn about our instructor training and center development programs..

Website
Kidpower Resources for Personal Safety Problems

We provide many free articles and resources on our website. You can learn more about these specific personal safety issues by visiting the following pages:
- **Bullying Prevention:** http://www.kidpower.org/ bullying.html
- **Child Abuse Prevention:** http://www.kidpower.org/child-abuse.html
- **Stranger Safety/Kidnapping Prevention:**
   http://www.kidpower.org/child-abduction.html

FREE E-newsletter

Kidpower e-newsletters provide readers with ideas and skills for increasing their safety and confidence through better communication, advocacy, and self-protection. Kidpower e-newsletters are full of useful articles and safety tips for protecting children, teens, and adults; inspiring real-life success stories; practical information for how to bring People Safety skills to others; timely responses to upsetting news events; reviews of books and videos; practices to build better relationships; training opportunities; and information on new publications and local services. To subscribe: http://www.kidpower.org/resources/e-newsletter.html

FREE Online Library

Our on-line free Library offers a wealth of articles about "People Safety" concepts and skills for children, teens and adults; videos; audio podcasts; a coloring book, and our blog. http://www.kidpower.org/resources/index.html

Kidpower Store

Our store offers publications for sale including e-books, Safety Comics, Teaching Kits, and Training Manuals.

Kidpower Safety Comics for Adults with Kids Ages 3-10. The tools in this comic book are most appropriate for parents, teachers, and other caregivers introducing "People Safety" to children ages 3 to 10 who are usually with adults who can help them. However, the skills are important for people of any age - adults too!

Kidpower Safety Comics for Adults with Kids Ages 9-13. The tools in this comic book are most appropriate for parents, teachers, and other caregivers introducing "People Safety" to children ages 9 to 13 who are beginning to be more independent in the world. However, the skills are important for people of any age – adults too!

Fullpower Safety Comics: The Fullpower Safety Comics is a cartoon-illustrated introduction to personal safety skills for teens and adults in basic language. The humorous black-and-white drawings provide an entertaining explanation of basic skills that will protect people's emotional and physical safety most of the time.

Kidpower Guide for Parents and Teachers eBook This 100-page eBook gives the reader an introduction to to the Kidpower program, including many of our stories and skills describing the Kidpower approach to protecting children from difficult and dangerous situations with strangers, peers, and familiar adults. This book is available in English or Spanish.

The Kidpower Teaching Kit. The Kidpower Teaching Kit is a set of five manuals using black-and-white cartoons and simple language to explain personal safety concepts and skills in an age-appropriate way. The focus is on children ages 3 to 8, but is relevant for any children who are not old enough to be out on their own or to be left home alone.

Teenpower/Fullpower Teaching Kit for Teens and Adults. The Fullpower Teaching Kit is a set of six manuals using black-and-white cartoons and basic language to explain personal safety concepts and skills to teens and adults. The humorous stories and clear directions make it easy and fun to introduce and practice personal skills in classrooms and other group settings.

Kidpower Comprehensive Program Manual. This is the textbook for our instructor training program and explains the Kidpower method for helping students be successful while practicing self protection, advocacy, confidence, personal safety and physical self defense skills.

Teenpower/Fullpower Comprehensive Program Manual. This is the textbook for our instructor training program and explains the Kidpower method for helping students be successful while practicing self protection, advocacy, confidence, personal safety and physical self defense skills.

The Relationship Safety Handbook. This 250-page handbook is designed to be used by victims and potential victims of relationship violence, as well as the support people in their lives. Support staff at organizations serving people at risk of, and those who have suffered from, relationship and domestic violence, can use this book as a tool to foster the integration of Kidpower's 'People Safety' skills into their everyday work.

An Invitation
From Irene

The reason I do this work is because, in 1985, in a public place with people standing all around, I protected a group of young children, including my seven-year-old daughter and my four-year-old son, from a man who was threatening to kidnap them. I stopped him by yelling and by ordering a bystander to help. The kids were fine, because what they saw was that I yelled and the bad guy ran away.

But I wasn't fine. I kept worrying. What if that man hadn't left? I knew I'd have done best to try to stop him, but what if he'd knocked me down? What if he even touched one of those children? And what about the unprotected children that he went on to harm?

Kidpower was born out of my search for answers to these questions. At first, I just wanted to know how to protect my own children. And then I wanted them to know how to protect themselves. And finally, I became determined that all children - and indeed all people – would have the skills and knowledge they needed to keep themselves and their loved ones safe.

Kidpower was established as a nonprofit organization in 1985, and thanks to the support and commitment of many exceptional people, we have now served over 1.2 million children, teens, and adults, including those with special needs, locally and around the world.

During our early years, although I knew the skills we were teaching could save children from terrible experiences, at first I was shy about asking for people to donate to Kidpower.

When I explained this to a friend who is a philanthropist and fundraiser, he said, "What if any of us saw a child being harmed? We would want to help that child. Helping Kidpower is a way of helping that child. So, you are just going to need to get over it, Irene!"

And then tragically, in 1993, twelve -year-old Polly Klaas was kidnapped from her home in a small town in northern California. Kidpower received an award from the families and friends of Polly Klaas for the workshop we did to for them. During that workshop, one of the girls said, "If we had had these skills, Polly would still be with us."

I knew that my shyness about marketing and fundraising was a luxury that I could no longer afford. Since then, I have dedicated my life to helping kids and other vulnerable people be safe from bullying, abuse, and other kinds of violence. And I will not stop until I am confident everyone has skills to be safe or has caring adults who are willing and prepared to help them learn those skills.

All of our services, including this book, are thanks to the gifts of time, money, and expertise from thousands of people like you who decided to contribute to Kidpower. I invite you to join us in fulfilling our vision of working together to build cultures of caring, respect, and safety for everyone, everywhere.

You have done the most important thing already by reading this book. I hope using these ideas and skills will give you useful tools for protecting the children in your life from bullying and other dangers.

I hope you will also see Kidpower as an important charity to support. It is often very difficult for people to make learning safety skills a priority in their lives, and we have found that it is through word of mouth that these skills spread. So, if you have found this book of value to you, please let other people know about the work we do. Tell your friends, family and co-workers. Show people skills you have learned and encourage them to learn more.

We are not supported by big government grants; we are supported by individuals just like you. We provide a tremendous amount of service with a very small and dedicated staff. But, we need your support to continue to proactively reach out to people deeply in need of our services – people in homeless and domestic violence shelters, children in developing countries living or working on the streets, and children and families being targeted for violence due to prejudice.

In our twenty-one years as an organization, we have never turned anyone away for lack of money. We want these skills to be accessible to everyone, everywhere. We believe everyone has the right to feel safe. Everyone deserves to live free of bullying, assault, abuse. Kidpower is working to give individuals, families, teachers, schools, and communities the skills to help make this happen. And, you can help.

Help support us by:
• Making a donation. Whether you can give a little or a lot, every gift counts! A donation of $50 provides services to a family in need. A donation of $100 gives hands-on teaching materials for a teacher or social worker. A donation of $500 trains a whole classroom of children.

• Buying a book for your friends and family. When you bring these skills to the people in your life, you help to create a shared language of safety that helps to create a culture of caring, respect and safety in your own personal community.

• Organizing a coaching session or workshop for the people important to you. Please contact us to learn more at safety@kidpower.org

• Telling others where to find us. Direct people to our website: www. kidpower.org.

• Staying in touch. Sign up to be a friend of ours on Facebook. Follow us on Twitter. Watch our safety videos on YouTube.

To be completely honest, it is still really hard for me to ask for money or support. But, I also know that Kidpower teaches people to advocate for themselves and others – and we need to do the same for our organization.

If you feel that Kidpower is of value to you and will be of value to others, please give as generously as you can. We are a small enough organization that I still personally see each donation that comes in. My heart soars and my eyes fill with tears when we get an unexpectedly generous gift, because I know what that money translates into – one more confident child, one more family, one more school, one more community we can help.

I thank you for your support and commitment to the safety of children and people everywhere.

Irene

A Tapestry Woven by Many Different Hands

The story of each person who has made a significant contribution to the Kidpower program would create a book unto itself. Kidpower is truly a tapestry of many different threads woven by many different hands. To learn more about the remarkable people who are responsible for the creation, development, and leadership of our organization, please visit: http://www. kidpower.org/about-us/tapestry.html

Photograph Credits

Cate Gaffney (photos on pages 31, 56, 131, and 137).
Catherine Arnold (photos on pages 19, 32, 117, and 125).
Cornelia Baumgartner (photo on page 112).
Juliana S.M. Piovanotti (photos on pages 14 and 75).

ISBN # 978-0-9796191-0-6

We Need Help!

Kidpower Teenpower Fullpower International is a charitable nonprofit organization. All of our services are gifts from others who came before you. Thanks to our Donors, we can offer free educational resources through our online Library; have our publications and workshops cost far less than they would otherwise; and create and offer services to those who are most vulnerable.

Please help us grow The Gift of Kidpower by becoming part of our 1,000 Donors Campaign. Whether you can give a few dollars or alot, YOUR gift counts!

We Want to Hear From You

We appreciate your reading this book and hope this information is useful for you. What worked well for you? How can we make this better? Do you have any unanswered questions? What about stories you'd like to share? Here's how to get in touch:

Kidpower Teenpower Fullpower International
www.kidpower.org
safety@kidpower.org
(o) 1-831-426-4407 Ext. 1#
Toll Free in US 1-800-467-6997 Ext. 1#

Made in the USA
San Bernardino, CA
28 January 2019